Adaptive User Interfaces

Computers and People Series

Edited by
B. R. GAINES and A. MONK

Adaptive User Interfaces

Edited by

DERMOT BROWNE

*KPMG Peat Marwick Management Consultants
231 Blackfriars Road, London, SE1, UK*

PETER TOTTERDELL

*MRC Social and Applied Psychology Unit,
Department of Psychology, University of Sheffield,
Sheffield, S10 2TN, UK*

MIKE NORMAN

*Department of Computer Science,
University of Hull, Hull, HU6 7RX, UK*

ACADEMIC PRESS

Harcourt Brace Jovanovich, Publishers
London   San Diego   New York
Boston   Sydney   Tokyo   Toronto

ACADEMIC PRESS LTD.
24/28 Oval Road,
London NW1 7DX

United States Edition published by
ACADEMIC PRESS INC.
San Diego, California 92101-4311

British Library Cataloguing in Publication Data

Is available

ISBN 0-12-137755-5

Printed in Great Britain by St Edmundsbury Press Ltd,
Bury St Edmunds, Suffolk

Contents

Contributors
Preface

Authors

Editors

Dermot Browne is now Executive Consultant at KPMG Peat Marwick Management Consultants, London and was formerly Technical Consultant at Data Logic, Harrow.

Peter Totterdell is Research Officer at the MRC/ESRC Social and Applied Psychology Unit, University of Sheffield, and was formerly Senior Research Engineer at STC Technology Ltd, Harlow.

Mike Norman is Rank Xerox Professor of Information Technology in the Department of Computer Science at Hull University.

Contributors

Stewart Anderson is a Lecturer in Computer Science at Edinburgh University and was formerley Lecturer in Computer Science at Heriott Watt University.

Ebby Adhami is a Consultant with Ernst & Young, London and was formerly Technical Consultant at Data Logic, Harrow.

Liz Boyle is a Research Fellow at the Human Communication Research Centre, Glasgow and was formerly Research Associate at the Scottish HCI Centre.

Paul Rautenbach is a Project Engineer at Computer Vision, Cambridge working on CAD/CAM systems and was previously Senior Research Engineer at STC Technology Ltd, Harlow.

Dave Riches is Senior Software Engineer at STC Technology Ltd, Harlow and was formerly Senior Research Officer at Essex University.

Alan Wilkinson is Senior Research Engineer at STC Technology Ltd, Harlow.

Preface

It is widely believed that "everyone should be computer literate" and as a consequence vast human and financial resources are being expended internationally on training individuals to adapt to using computers within their lives. The premise of the research that is reported in this volume is that "computers should be user literate". Comparatively small resources have been devoted to building flexibility into computers; flexibility which would enable computers to adapt to the diverse needs of the individuals who use them.

The research reported here was part of a project which looked at the problem of designing adaptive computer interfaces. An adaptive computer intereface is one which can change its behaviour to suit the individual or group using it. This can range from an interface which switches fonts to suit the preference of a user, to an interface which builds and evaluates a model of the user in order to improve the effectiveness of communication between the computer and the user.

The Adaptive Intelligent Dialogues project, also known as the AID project, was a four-year project which researched and developed techniques for designing and building adaptive computer interfaces. The AID project was part of the United Kingdom's Advanced Technology Alvey Programme. The collaborators on the project were: STC Technology Ltd, Data Logic Ltd, British Telecommunications plc, The University of Hull, The University of Strathclyde and The University of Essex.

Special mention should go to the project managers Phil O'Donovan and his successor Paul Cooper of STC Technology Ltd who managed to keep the project on course. We would also like to thank Tom Stewart of System Concepts Ltd who was the external monitor for the project. His contributions at workshops were always very positive, apt and well received.

We would like to acknowledge the contribution of all those that worked on the project, whether it was for four weeks or four years. In keeping with the spirit of the venture, we will simply list their names without mentioning affiliation, position or time on the project:

Ebby Adhami, Jim Alty, Bruce Anderson, Stuart Anderson, Farhat Arshad, Bob Benton, Len Botacci, Peter Boucherat, Liz Boyle, Pamela Brody, Andrew Brooks, Dermot Browne, Nigel Cliffe, Ian Clowes, Gilbert Cockton, Ian Cole, Stephanie Cookson, Martin Cooper, Paul Cooper, Tony Cox, Colin Davenport, Graham Dunkling, Tony Fountain, John Friend, Andrew Hockley, Colin Hopkins, Bernard Horan, Safwan J'Affra, Peter Jones, Neil Lawrence, Richard Lawrence, Graham Leedham, Pat Leisner, Hamid Lesan, Andrew Marshall, Terry Mayes, Phil McEachen, Swapan Mitra, Linda Moxey, Dave Moynaghan, Brian Murphy, Mike Norman, Phil O'Donovan, Robin Pyburn, Paul Rautenbach, Dave Riches, Colin Robertson, Osnat Ron, Nigel Seel, Briun Sharratt, Andrew Stewart, Mike Thornton, Peter Totterdell, Robert Trevellyan, Alan Wilkinson, Romualdas Viliunas, Albert Wong.

We would also like to acknowledge the support provided by Alvey and SERC in part funding the AID project. STC Technology would also like to acknowledge International Computers Ltd for their support.

One caveat, although much reference is made to work from within the project, the thoughts and ideas expressed here are the responsibility of the editors and authors alone and do not necessarily reflect the views of all the individuals and organisations involved in the project. Some of the ideas reported here have been reported elsewhere - in papers, journals, workshops and conferences - but this volume is intended to bring together the results of the project under one cover.

It is hoped that the work will be of interest to anyone who is seriously interested in Human Computer Interaction; both the issues and the practice.

Chapter 1
Introduction

P. Totterdell

The following chapter is an introduction to the Adaptive Intelligent Dialogues (AID) project which was the source of the research reported in this book. The chapter begins by describing the objectives, participants, and development of the project. During the course of the project a number of adaptive interfaces appeared as a result of work outside the project. Some of these interfaces are briefly reviewed in this chapter. The editors then describe what it is they hope to achieve by disseminating the results of the AID project to a wider audience, and hence they describe what you the reader might hope to gain. The chapter ends with a brief summary of the contents and rationale of other chapters.

This book is the result of a four-year collaborative venture between three industrial and three academic partners who, with the help of government funds, allowed a group of researchers to tackle the problem of designing adaptive user interfaces for computers. An adaptive user interface is an interface which can change its behaviour to suit an individual or group of individuals.

Our account concentrates on the technical outcomes of this venture but an equally interesting account could have described the sociological development of a project of this type. Indeed we might have chosen to illustrate the processes of adaptation by referring to the course of change within the project itself. But we start more mundanely with some details of the project.

The AID Project

The Adaptive Intelligent Dialogues (AID) project was part of the United Kingdom's Advanced Technology Alvey program which sponsored collaborative computing and information technology projects involving both industry and academia in the UK. The AID project was the largest project of the Man-Machine Interface (MMI) section of the Alvey programme. The project ran from October 1984 to September 1988. The collaborators on the project were: STC Technology Ltd, Data Logic Ltd, British Telecommunications plc, The University of Hull, The University of Strathclyde and The University of Essex.

The project was originally set up to "research the techniques appropriate to the development of user interfaces that adapt to a particular user's ability and knowledge of a given system". The term adaptive referred both to self adaptive and user tailored systems (terms which will be explored in depth later on). The justification for the project was that with computers becoming more widespread and having to accommodate a wider range of users, it was no longer satisfactory for designers to aim the level of interaction at an average user because nobody conformed to the stereotype of the average user.

The specific objectives of the project were to:

i) Research the principles underlying intelligent adaptive interaction.

ii) Build software exemplars to demonstrate this research.

iii) Evaluate the effectiveness of the exemplars.

iv) Produce tools to assist in developing adaptive user interfaces.

The project was divided into three phases. The first phase developed an adaptive interface to an electronic mail system using the (at the time) state-of-the-art tools and techniques. The second phase of the project researched the key issues of adaptive interaction. As well as producing theoretical frameworks for understanding adaptation, the second phase also produced a number of software exemplars. The third phase of the project consolidated the research by building improved exemplars which illustrated general techniques for constructing adaptive interfaces. The final phase also developed tools to facilitate future development of adaptive interfaces.

Phase 1

Phase 1 of the project designed and built an adaptive front end to the British Telecom electronic mail system Telecom Gold. It was hoped that the existing interface to the application would provide a suitable baseline against which to measure the performance of the adaptive interface. The application also had the advantage that it was a "real world" rather than a "toy" application and would therefore be a good test of the adequacy of current Human Computer Interface (HCI) wisdom and computer technology.

The adaptive interface was built in a single design, build and test cycle, with no opportunity for redesign. A description of the interface architecture and its components can be found in later chapters but essentially it comprised a dialogue controller (which interacted with the user), a user model and an application expert. The application expert interfaced the whole system to the application via a modem. The phase 1 system adapted along a number of dimensions, the most important of which was the level of help it gave a user. The system was effective in as much as it provided user assistance related to user competence, but this was at the expense of unacceptably high response times.

It has been said that the sum of the components in the phase 1 system was greater than the whole. And certainly one of the successes of the system was the design of the application expert. With hindsight one might question whether the design effort required to interface the system via a slow and noisy telephone line to an application with unknown states might have been better spent on designing the user interface to an easier application. But as with any research, the spinoffs are often as valuable as they are unanticipated; and the application expert was a valuable spinoff.

Evaluation of the phase 1 system proved difficult and it became apparent that adaptation is of superficial value unless the non-adaptive components of an interface are also of sufficient design quality. In an effort to make a controlled comparison with a non-adaptive version of the interface, the designers of the phase 1 system had neglected this requirement and had built adaptive facilities on top of a rather poor user interface.

Phase 2

Phase 2 of the project ran from January 1986 to September 1987. The original objective for phase 2 had been to produce a commercially viable exemplar. However, following the experience of phase 1, it was clear that phase 2 needed to address some very fundamental issues concerning the characteristics and classification of adaptive systems. This included looking at the use of the concept of adaptation in other disciplines such as biology and cybernetics, and led on to a clarification of its usage within the field of HCI.

In phase 2 adaptation took on the meaning of an approach to design rather than being seen as a universal architecture. In particular it was viewed as a framework for deferring design decisions. A theory- based approach to the design and evaluation of adaptive systems via metrics also emerged in this phase.

It was decided after a few months of the phase that the project needed a single domain for its exemplars and experiments. This was seen as a way of bringing various strands of work together. The project chose document preparation as its domain because it seemed to offer problems requiring adaptive solutions. The exemplars which followed seemed to offer alternatives to the cognitive user modelling approach which had dominated the first phase. They demonstrated that in some cases adaptation can be provided without a sophisticated model of the user. This is important given that the bandwidth of communication between user and interface is sometimes too narrow to justify an elaborate user model.

Phase 3

The final phase of the project used the groundwork of phase 2 to produce improved exemplars. Again the exemplars were within the domain of document preparation and they were chosen to illustrate more general techniques for constructing adaptive interfaces. The exemplars showed considerable diversity in their demonstration of adaptation. For example: the Task Organiser adapted to linguistic context, Groupie 2 adapted to the help preferences of a community of users, Reference Information Provider adapted to relevance, and Adaptive Menu Structure adapted to frequency of use. These exemplars as well as others are described in later chapters, especially Chapter 5.

Phases 1 and 2 had shown that it was hard to identify user or task variability, the sources for adaptation, in the course of using conventional system design techniques. What was needed was a method of systematically assessing situation specific requirements to see whether or not they could profitably be realised at run-time by an adaptive interface. The method also needed to address the practicality of using an adaptive solution. The computer has only limited access to the user's situation and can therefore only detect and monitor a limited set of stimuli. A method called MAID (Methodology for Adaptive Interface Design) was developed to satisfy these needs. This was complemented by using the evaluation experiences of the project to devise a detailed protocol for formative and summative evaluation of adaptive interfaces.

Phase 3 also delivered some tools to support the construction of adaptive interfaces. The ideas of application modelling developed in phase 1 were later incorporated into a tool (HIFI) for integrating user interface design with system functionality. And two other tools, Deferred Design Tool (DDT) and Task Description Language (TDL) were developed to support the project's design method.

Management

Research on the scale of the AID project requires good management. Whilst good management cannot guarantee success to a research project, bad management usually guarantees failure. And in as much as the results reported here are a measure of success or failure, it may be of use to record some of the conditions which were the context for that outcome.

The work of the project was divided into "workpackages" with personnel from different sites participating in workpackages which accorded with their interests. Meetings to organise these workpackages were arranged as necessary. Every quarter year a review workshop was held for all staff on the project. The responsibility for organising workshops rotated around sites. The workshops were an opportunity for discussing general progress on the project and for organising the following three months of work.

Management meetings were held on a monthly basis and involved a project manager from each site. These meetings gave way to technical management meetings in the later stages of the project. These involved more junior and technical interested representatives from each site. The project was reviewed internally by a monitoring officer chosen every three months from the staff of the site organising the next workshop. Externally the project was reviewed both by an independent monitoring officer who attended project workshops and reported to the funding body, and also by major review with an Alvey Committee at the end of each phase.

The three phases of the project were important in structuring the research. Phase 1 of the project, as well as providing valuable technical insights, also served to facilitate collaboration within the project. Working in cross site design teams to tight deadlines on concrete problems undoubtedly helped to break down organisation barriers. Evidence of this cohesiveness came from workshop guests who commented that they could not tell who came from which site. The only drawback, however, to this style of research is that it discourages divergence and it prevented the project tackling fundamental questions until phase 2.

In contrast, the more *laissez faire* style in the initial stages of phase 2 meant that there was little prospect of integrating the various lines of work that were happening at different sites. And some of the work was on the margins of usefulness to the central adaptive interface problem. Hence, the decision to choose a common problem domain ie document preparation.

In the project's original conception, it was envisaged that the industrial partners would contribute their experience and expertise of system building to the project whilst the academic partners would contribute more to the theory and evaluation issues. In reality this proved to be an artificial separation. Much of the "thinking" came from the industrialist and much of the "building" from the academics. In part this was a reflection of recruitment outcomes at the different sites. But perhaps it also exposes the myth of the industrial/academic stereotypes.

A project of the size and length of AID develops its own culture in the form of personal allegiances, schools and even generations of thought. Only a small core of researchers were part of the project throughout its duration and even then the project occupied a varying percentage of their time. A full list of the people that worked on the project is given at the start of the book. It would be an interesting exercise to look at how their individual interests and time on the project shaped its course.

Collaboration on a project such as AID should not be measured simply in terms of its deliverables. Some of the other benefits include:

The acquisition of a wider skill base for participants.

Increased contacts in relevant fields and communities.

An increase in status for collaborative groups within their own organisations.

Increased recruitment of skilled human factors staff.

A wider awareness and appreciation of human factors issues.

The increased adoption of a user centred design process within the organisations.

However collaboration does have its costs, particularly in terms of its resource intensity and administrative overheads.

Other Adaptive Interfaces

The AID project proposal recognised that adaptiveness is required in the interface because no single fixed solution is suitable for all users or even one user over a period of time or range of applications. The interface needs to adapt to the user's changing skills and requirements, and the assistance provided by the system needs to be relevant to the tasks the user is performing. This requirement for adaptive interfaces had been recognised for some time (e.g. Edmonds, 1982) and yet there have been relatively few examples of adaptive interfaces. Here we provide a brief review of the work of others in this area and name some of the interfaces which do exist.

Edmonds (1982) described three modes of adaptation: adaptation by a specialist, adaptation by a trained user, and adaptation by any user. The SYNICS system (Edmonds and Guest, 1978) translates strings according to specified transformational rules and is an example of a system which can be used in the first mode, for example to allow a specialist to produce alternative error messages. Edmonds also gives early examples of systems in the other modes. All of these modes are examples of tailorable systems, that is they are adapted by something outside the system whether it be the designer or user. But Edmonds also introduced the concept of a self-adaptive interface.

A self adaptive interface changes automatically in response to its experience with users. Three types of self-adaptive interface were distinguished. Those which collect information about the user and tailor the interface responses either during a session or between sessions. Those which identify a user as belonging to a particular category and set the interface's parameters accordingly (once only). And those in which the interface doesn't change but performance improves, for example by dealing with errors more quickly. Early examples of all three types are given by Edmonds. Innocent (1982) also described some of the basic principles of self adaptive user interfaces. He gave a possible architecture for a self adaptive user interface incorporating an expert modifier which monitors and evaluates user and system behaviour with the purpose of reshaping the 'soft facade' of the interface.

Some of the adaptive interfaces to appear in recent years include the following:

Connect (Alty, 1984a). Connect is an adaptable dialogue delivery vehicle that achieves adaptability through a production system which monitors user interaction and consequently opens or closes arcs in the dialogue network.

Dialog (Maskery, 1984). Maskery undertook some experiments with an adaptive interface to a package of statistical tools called Dialog. The interface had three levels of dialogue, forced choice system led, free choice system led, and free choice user led. Users experienced difficulties when they were transferred to the user led interface.

Adaptable help manual (Mason & Thomas, 1984). The adaptive part of the interface models the user by quantifying their experience of the system using a weighted set of user descriptive variables. The model then determines what type of help should be retrieved for the user.

Monitor (Benyon, 1984). Monitor selects dialogue scripts based on information about the user collected in a user model. For example, the user model records whether or not a user has performed a task before and a more verbose script is selected if the user has not previously performed the task. The prototype of Monitor was in the domain of computer assisted learning but its design was intended to be general purpose. LS-1 (Smith, 1984) uses a genetic algorithm to learn a set of problem solving heuristics. It has been applied to the problems of simple maze walking and draw poker, and has been shown to improve its performance over time in both domains. Its performance at draw poker was better than another program judged to perform at the same level as an experienced human player.

Pal (Pickering *et al.*, 1984). Pal is a communication aid for the disabled which adapts by predicting the stems of words being typed by the user. By allowing the user to accept its predictions it is able to reduce the length of the keying sequence.

Poise (Croft, 1984). The Poise system provides assistance to the users of an office system based on models of office tasks. Poise infers users' tasks from their actions and provides context sensitive assistance.

Document retrieval (Croft, 1984). The document retrieval system uses associative search networks (ASN) which work on feedback from the user to change the set of weights on the system's search strategies.

Experiments have shown that the ASN reliably learns to select the appropriate strategy.

Personalised directory (Greenberg & Witten, 1985). Greenberg and Witten constructed an interface to a menu driven telephone directory system. The interface reduced selection time and error rate by ordering the menus according to the probability of selection which was based on the user's frequency of retrieval for each number.

Adaptive indexing (Furnas, 1985). This system monitors the words that a community of users employ to refer to system objects. It then increases the weight of association between the words and the objects. Where necessary it adds new words to the index. In this way the system increases its chance of successfully recognising subsequent user commands.

We will meet some of these systems again in Chapter 3 when we start to classify adaptive systems.

Aims

Who is this book aimed at? Firstly, it is intended to help anyone that might be considering designing an adaptive interface. Inevitably any such person will cross many of the same hurdles that we did. For example, we had long debates on: the distinction between and relative merits of user tailored and self adaptive interfaces; what is and what isn't an adaptive interface (a very slippery slope this one); good HCI vs adaptation; the best architecture for an adaptive interface; the domain specifity of results; appropriate evaluation procedures etc. Hopefully this book will help to lower those hurdles through its description of frameworks, techniques and experimental results.

The book should appeal not only to those looking for an adaptive solution to a problem but also to anyone that is interested in learning more about the issues and techniqes of HCI. The techniques required for an adaptive interface commonly apply also to non adaptive interfaces. HCI has often been seen to be about building fancy interface gadgets or about choosing screen colours. It is neither ; it is a serious design activity. And designing adaptive interfaces are part of that activity.

At the start of the project, adaptation was seen as something which could be packaged together and bolted on to a system. It was to be an extra facility, something which would differentiate the system from its market competitiors. However, it became clear that adaptation was much more part of the design process than it was a product in itself.

Adaptive mechanisms have evolved to play an important role in human physiology, e.g. the adaptation of the circadian system to changes in environmental time (Hildebrant and Moog, 1988). Adaptive behaviour is also critical in successful human to human interaction. It is perhaps not unreasonable, therefore, to think that successful interaction between computer and human will also require the computer system to exhibit adaptive behaviour. In humans the long term outcome of failure to adapt is disease (Mackay, 1984). There may come a time when we refer to computers which don't adapt as diseased. On this count we have some very unhealthy computers at present! The same preconditions and symptoms of failure to adapt that we identify in humans, such as life event changes, stressors, coping behaviour and health status may also begin to apply to computers. But that is for the future.

We end this particular chapter with an overview of the chapters that follow. But first an apology. Much of the terminology in the field of HCI is used very loosely. Sometimes terms are used interchangeably and sometimes they are used to make distinctions. We haven't helped this situation. For example, we sometimes refer to adaptation as if it were a thing not a process, despite the claim that it is the latter. It is awkward to do otherwise. We also use "interface" and "system" interchangeably. "Methods", "models" and "techniques" too. Probably others. Hopefully the reader will be able to understand our use of terms within the context (we rely on your adaptive capabilities). We have, however, made an effort to restrict ourselves to using the term "adaptation" rather than "adaption". But others in the field also use adaption (Edmonds, 1982).

Overview

Chapter 2. John Bloggs is a rather unpleasant fictional character who employed a team of extremely pleasant user interface designers to provide an adaptive interface. His story illustrates some of the problems and benefits of adaptive user interfaces. Some of these problems can be solved by using the frameworks described in the chapter. There are frameworks for: identifying differences in the end user population that might be reasons for using adaptation; identifying the purposes or likely benefits that might be obtained; and identifying changes that could be made to the interface. A set of metrics and a methodology for designing adaptive interfaces are then described.

Chapter 3. This chapter takes a step back from the practicalities of designing adaptive interfaces to adopt a theoretical stance on the problem. Adaptation is viewed as a set of alternative design choices for relating a system to its environment. The game "Prisoner's Dilemma" is used to construct a taxonomy of adaptive system design, within which current adaptive systems are classified. Some parallels with evolution are noted and the implications for designers are described. A general architecture for adaptive systems is then inferred from this view of adaptation.

Chapter 4. An interface designer will need to know what methods are available to support the design of an adaptive (or non adaptive) interface. Chapter 4 reviews these methods under the headings of user models, dialogue models, task models and application models. These methods are not restricted to adaptive interfaces and the text should therefore also provide a useful review of the current status of methods in HCI. The specific relevance of a method to adaptive interface design is highlighted where necessary. The application expert of the AID phase 1 system is described in considerably more detail than other methods. This is not because we feel that it is more important than the alternatives (well, perhaps we do!) but because it is a result of the project and therefore needs fuller reporting.

Chapter 5. The methods described in Chapter 4 were general to interface design but could be used as components of an adaptive interface. In contrast, this chapter looks specifically at techniques for providing adaptation at an interface. This includes: genetic algorithms, adaptive scheduling, pattern matching, context and user models. Most of these are illustrated by examples from the AID project. The chapter begins by taking another look at architecture, and shows how three exemplars conform to the general architecture described in Chapter 3. The chapter finishes on two specific issues, namely adaptation to a group of users and the weighting of evidence.

Chapter 6. Interface designers ought to be able to show that the techniques they are using are of benefit to the user and that they are an improvement on other techniques. This chapter describes the evaluation methods that can be used to evaluate the performance of an adaptive interface. It also describes evaluation methods that can be used to support the design process itself. Many of the methods have been developed to deal specifically with adaptive interfaces, but most will also apply to the evaluation of non adaptive interfaces.

Chapter 7. This chapter summarises some of the lessons of the AID project and looks into the crystal ball for the future of adaptive interfaces.

Chapter 2
Why Build Adaptive Systems?

D. Browne, M. Norman and D. Riches

Two major assumptions underly the building of any adaptive system. Firstly, that there are differences in the end-user population that can provide good REASON for adaptation. Secondly, that there is some PURPOSE or benefit to be obtained. It is insufficient to describe the purpose as one of improving the user interface of the system. Further, given the identifiable user differences and that they can form the basis for purposeful adaptive change, the question remains as to what those changes should actually be? Finally, discussion will turn to the adoption of a suitable methodology for developing adaptive systems.

To provide a context for later discussion this chapter begins with the story of a fictional character. John Bloggs suffered the consequences of having a poorly designed non-adaptive system and sought the skills of user interface designers specialising in adaptive techniques. The assumptions and many of the problems of commissioning an adaptive user interface are found in this story.

A TALE OF RESERVED SUCCESS

My name is John Bloggs and I am head of a Communications Department for a large industrial company. The personnel in my department use electronic mail to convey short messages to our company's subsidiaries around the country. The work is boring, tedious, monotonous and I'm a miserable boss so there is a rather high turnover of staff. In fact, no one lasts more than a fortnight in my department. Nonetheless, I am interested in increasing the rate of message passing although I don't give a damn about staffing issues. Thus it has come to pass that a research project will be undertaken to investigate and recommend a means of increasing productivity.

A number of entities in my department seem crucial to the whole system. Firstly there is the hardware and software being utilised and secondly there are the people who are employed in the department. The only part of the system that is open to overt change is the Human-Computer Interface (HCI). Thus, it was decided that the research project would concentrate on the characteristics of the HCI and its relation to the system's users. The first exercise undertaken was an analysis of the interaction between user and computer. This included the collection of protocols of system usage. These showed that staff, still in their first week with the department, passed 50% less messages than staff in their second week with the department. My first thought was to get rid of all new staff but I was bright enough to realise that within a week no messages would be being passed at all. Further analysis showed that the less experienced staff were spending 20% of their time reading the system manuals. This highlighted exactly what I should do. Hide the manuals. This I did, but to my surprise work throughput dropped by 34%. At this stage I was stumped and decided to call in the AID team.

I'd heard of this group from my friend who had met the team's leader at an "Open Day" at the Department of Trade and Industry.

The work they were doing sounded astonishing. Creating computer systems that understood their users and were able to help the most computer illiterate people do a good day's graft. Exactly what I wanted. A quick phone call set the wheels of progress in motion. A meeting was arranged with a formidable subset of the AID team called the Adaptation Working Group. At this meeting I was informed that my problem was nothing unusual, but still of great interest. At last someone was willing to listen to me. In exchange for the case study material they were willing to provide the techniques and resources to realise my ambitions for productivity. Their first piece of advice was to get the manuals back out of the cupboard and sure enough work throughput reached its previous level. I was impressed.

At this point the AID team started talking measurements and objectives, of which I had many. The first measurement they made was of the paltry work throughput that was being achieved. This seemed sensible enough, but then they started discussing, in some sort of clandestine language, about the characteristics of the message passing system and something they referred to as adaptation. I asked more questions but the answers didn't convince me until they said they could demonstrate their beliefs in terms of further measurements.

More time was invested in the AID team and they went to work. They talked about theories, heuristics, user modelling, user characteristics, application characteristics and particularly about trade-offs because of the department's high staff turnover. Then they came up with a proposal just in time for my summer holidays. On the basis of the work of Alias Smith & Jones (1969), and the TT and more T & T company, they proposed that an adaptive HCI be provided. The HCI characteristic that would change would be the help messages, in particular the information content of these messages. Information content being measured in terms of total number of concepts (commands, arguments, objects) contained in the message. The obvious question was how do you know when to change the level of information in a message? "Well," the AID team said, "there is a relationship between the amount of information required and the amount of errors a user makes. What we wish to do is decrease users' error rates more quickly than they would normally decrease."

At this point I was flabbergasted and dismayed. I wanted to increase work throughput and they were trying to decrease errors. They eased my worries by saying that a decrease in error rate would cause an increase in work throughput. Being far from convinced I cancelled my holiday and decided to follow the AID team's work more closely."What does it all mean?" The AID team explained. "We have the following data and theories at hand. With these we have the beginnings of a complete picture of what you really require Mr Bloggs."

> RATE OF WORK THROUGHPUT. This is the measure of your system's success. Your objective, and the benefit the system aims to provide, is increased work throughput. This can be achieved by reducing the error rate, or so we shall show.

Re-analysing the protocols provided data depicting the relationship between error rate and experience. And basically, our theory predicts that error rate can be decreased more quickly if the information content of help messages is increased whenever error rate increases.

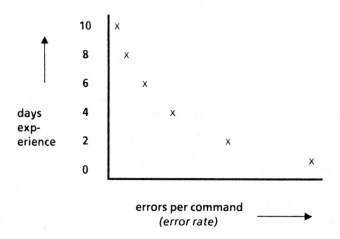

The AID team said quite candidly that they didn't know the relationship between information content and error rate only its general direction. The difficult bit for me to swallow came when they said they did not need to fully understand the relationship. At this point I was ready to sack and then sue the lot of them but I graciously gave them the opportunity to explain themselves. They said "it's all a matter of control theory."

"Tell me more" I said. "We know what we want to do, that is decrease errors,we know what we are going to change, that is the information content of help messages. All we have to do now is build a system that measures error rate, changes the level of information content accordingly, and then monitors its own success in order to optimise the information content so as to achieve a minimum error rate." "That sounds like another measurement to me," I said feeling like a part of the team. "Well in fact it's two more," they replied without thinking.

- Error rate while the system is operational.

    This is what we are trying to minimise by changing the information content of help messages.

- Information content as it is altered.

    This affords the opportunity to understand the relationship between information content and error rate.

"Of course it doesn't matter to you Mr Bloggs what the relationship between error rate and information content is, because the system will just optimise this as far as you are concerned. However we would like to understand this relationship so that we can write a few papers about it, and so that we learn how to build a similar system more quickly and better next time."

"We will also take some more measures in order to learn about the functioning of our software *in situ*. For instance, we would like to know whether our adaptive software is working efficiently. That is, how long does the software take to ascertain the relationship between error rate and information content and how much processing (time) does it take to make the appropriate adaptations. If we were performing individual user modelling then our measurements would include data for individual's error rates as well. In this way we might be able to say more about why it is useful."

Well I can tell you I went away on holiday with faith in my heart that the AID team were going to be successful in improving the work throughput of my department. I could almost feel a promotion coming on. When I returned I was not disappointed. Within a week of the new software coming on-line, throughput was up 10% and within another week it was up a staggering 30%. I was also pleasantly surprised that my staff turnover decreased but we will never know whether this was due to the AID team's work or because I became a pleasant boss.

The AID team were also pleased; they now understood the relationship between information content and error rate, and between error rate and work throughput. Over a few drinks to celebrate the success of the project I asked the AID team to tell me where else within the company the knowledge gained would be useful. "For instance," I said "could I impress the data processing department's manager by porting the adaptive software to the data entry system?" "Oh no," the answer quickly came back, "the data entry software doesn't have any help messages." "Well how about the electronic mail system in the accounts department?" "Oh no," was the reply again, "the staff in the accounts department don't use the system often enough." "Well how about in the R & D department, they are always using electronic mail?" "No, the problem with them is that their staff turnover is almost negligible, they probably wouldn't benefit from any such adaptation." "Well where else can I use it?" The AID team replied as one, "the only place we are sure you can use it, is when staff turnover is extremely high (average time with the company two weeks), users are utilising communications software for the duration of the working day and the actual software is MINAS 204; the same as your department uses." I thought for a moment and then said "from what you've just told me the adaptive software you have installed in my department won't even work there now that staff turnover has become much lower." "Yes, that's right, funny isn't it," said the AID team with a wry grin. "If we had the time to collect more data then we would be able to say under what circumstances our software would be generally applicable. We would need to identify the range of user characteristics and HCI characteristics within which it applied. It is a very complicated situation with many variables and dependencies."

This is John Bloggs once again staggered and dumbfounded by this tale of promise and reserved success.

This short story shows how the design of an adaptive system can only be progressed on the basis of specific knowledge. Knowledge of the differences between users or within users. In this case differences in user capability leading to observable differences in error rate. Also knowledge of why the adaptive system is being built, namely for the purpose of increasing operational speed. Any adaptive system must also be imbued with the means of meeting its purpose, in this case the monitoring of error rates as a basis for changing the information content of error messages.

The variability in individual differences, range of purposes that adaptive systems might be built to meet, and the range of "behaviours" that such a system might display are discussed in the following sections.

REASONS for Adaptation

The *raison d'être* of adaptive computer systems is primarily the acknowledgement that end-users are heterogeneous. In most production industries, this heterogeneity is made an implicit affector of design, certainly in terms of anthropometric heterogeneity. For instance, it would be foolish to design emergency exits such that the larger proportioned members of the population could not utilise them. And in seat design, it is important that the seat be comfortable to most members of the population. Studies documenting cultural and cross-cultural anthropometric dimensions can be used as reference during the design process. Nonetheless, it is always the case that a design will not meet usability criteria for every individual. Building tailorability into any one product increases its potential market but there are limitations as to how much flexibility can be incorporated into any one product. Alternatively, product ranges can be provided in order to reach more of the market. For instance, in the fashion industry, different sizes of the one product are manufactured in order to reach a wider market.

The situation is similar in the computer product industry. There is a market that is heterogenous and manufacturers want to provide systems that reach as large a market as possible. Unfortunately the diversity of end-users of computers is relevant to the manufacturer on more than simply physical dimensions. User-computer interaction has cognitive as well as mechanical elements. The very partaking of interaction affects the end-user in that their interpretation of events may affect future interaction.

Our aim is to cope with the heterogeneity between and within users by designing computer systems which can adapt their own functioning, at least at a communication level, in order to accommodate users throughout their interactions with the system. For this to become a reality, the dimensions of user variability that affect user-computer interaction need to be established.

INDIVIDUAL DIFFERENCES

There is no shortage of candidate dimensions of human variability that may impact computer usage. In fact bibliographies (Buie, 1986) of papers citing individual differences are emerging. Rather than attempting to document a complete list of candidate dimensions, we will simply review some alternative classifications followed by one generated by this project.

Noah & Halpin (1986) addressed the issue of providing adaptive user interfaces for planning and decision support applications in a military context. Their argument for adaptive user interfaces was that the effectiveness of users depends on their expertise on several dimensions of skill:

- The extent of an individual's model of automated data processing (ADP), including their comprehensions of conventions and prerequisites for human-machine dialogues.

- The extent of an individual's model of the particular support system. For instance, the user's familiarity with the system's range of functionality.

- The user's perceptual and psychomotor skills and the ability these afford the user for appropriate action and reaction.

- The user's problem-solving and pattern recognition capabilities as examples of the wide variety of cognitive skills.

- The user's ability to exploit their social and organisational situation.

- A user's capability to define goals, discriminate tasks, identify alternatives and essentially apply system capabilities to execute procedures.

- An individual's abilities in particular domains. Different domains are more or less pertinent to individuals.

All of these dimensions of variability could conceivably be bases for providing an adaptive user interface in order to improve end-user effectiveness. Such an interface would have to be supported by a dynamic internal model of the user's internal mental state and task environment.

Veer *et al.* (1985) proposed different dimensions of user variability when considering end-users performing non-specialist jobs as encountered in "open shop" situations, examples being general purpose office computer systems and a university computer centre. They concentrated on individual differences impinging on the gaining of experience. They believed these to be most relevant to novice and occasional users. These differences fall into two main categories, namely cognitive styles and personality factors.

Differences in cognitive style result from permanent dispositions such as levels of intelligence and enduring influences, such as culture and education. Field independence is one such style that has been extensively researched (Witkin & Goodenough, 1981). Field dependent persons are more influenced by context than field independent persons. As a result field dependent persons demonstrate a fixation to certain solutions with the effect that they have difficulty developing a necessarily different solution in similar situations to which the first applied. Another cognitive style dimension that can be usefully described is impulsivity/reflectivity. Reflective persons take more time than an impulsive person to proceed with a task. Thus impulsives make more errors, having drawn quicker conclusions on inadequately thought through premises. The third cognitive style dimension proposed is operation learning/comprehension learning. Basically, operational learners will attempt to derive rules and develop tools to aid interaction. Comprehension learning results in the assimilation of overviews. That is, general rules that apply across remote parts of a domain.

These two learning styles are not mutually exclusive. To become an all-round expert requires both styles of learning to be applied.

Veer *et al.* (1985) also proposed that a number of personality factors affect the gaining of experience. Personality factors are deemed as quite stable over time. Firstly, the dimension of introversion/ extraversion. Introverts tend to withdraw when stressed, whilst extraverts get bored and will withdraw in repetitive non-diverse situations. Thus extraverts will attempt new methods of working which may lead to mistakes. Users may also vary considerably in terms of "negative fear of failure". Those who are highly fearful may not act rationally in ill-structured situations. Perception of own competence is a further cognitive difference that may be worthy of consideration. Perceived heuristic competence will affect an individual's exploration of a system. Those who perceive themselves to have high heuristic competence will be more systematic than those who do not.

Simply taking two of the many authors who have proposed classifications of individual differences has generated a substantial list of candidate reasons for building adaptive user interfaces. Not surprisingly the AID project also generated a list of such reasons. These are somewhat more general than those described so far, and as a consequence encompass a larger set of individual differences.

Psycho-motor Skills

Noah & Halpin (1986) have referred to this category as a user's ability to respond appropriately to a stimulus. Obviously there are differences in a person's psycho-motor skills as demonstrated for instance, by different keying capabilities. Nonetheless, deriving implications from such differences is not straightforward. Differences may be most pertinent for computer driven supervisory and tracking tasks, but it is difficult to imagine how a system might adapt to ameliorate differences. Noah & Halpin suggest that displays and control surfaces might be modified in response to a user's performance, but they do not elaborate. The general relevance of this dimension may be limited but it is included for completeness. It is usually the case that individuals are hand picked for tasks requiring good psycho-motor skills. Nonetheless, adaptive systems have been developed for users with impaired motor skills. For instance,

Pickering *et al.* (1984) developed an adaptive system that capitalised on the redundancy of language to predi⸱⸱ user input through a keyboard. In this way the amount of keying required was reduced.

Capability

At any one time a user will possess a level of procedural expertise which may or may not enable the completion of tasks on a particular system. This dimension has been described and broken down in different ways by many authors. The value of classifying users on such a dimension is the subject of much debate (Koeffler, 1986). Often researchers find it convenient to classify users along this dimension using the three categories of novice, intermediate and expert (Alty, 1984a).

Schneider (1982) extends this further to include both a parrot category to describe someone who will repeat strings of commands without understanding them, and a master category as a stage beyond expert. He describes this five-stage classification as "prescriptive" and provides results indicating its value to designers of user interfaces. The general criticism levelled at those who categorise users in this fashion is that the dimension of capability is inevitably continuous rather than discrete. On practical grounds it must have limited value given that users will fall into different categories dependent on experience and practise. In addition, it must be remembered that individuals will have different levels of capability for alternative aspects of a system.

Rosson (1984), in a survey of text editor usage by programmers, non-programmer researchers and secretaries reported that the programmers spent more time customising their keyboard than did the latter categories of user. This and other similar findings were attributed to the prior experience of the different users with similar facilities and the capability this afforded them for the task of customisation.

Learning Ability

This quality determines a user's attainment of understanding. Individuals have various dispositions towards gaining understanding of different types of concepts. This is the basis of many psychometric tests designed to predict future performance at specific tasks. The works of Piaget (1955) strongly suggest that individuals attain different levels of cognitive functioning that dispose them to gaining different levels of understanding.

Given that differences in learning ability most directly effect attainment of understanding the most salient application area for capitalising on the difference is Computer Aided Instruction software. Learning tasks can be considered hierarchically with the attainment of higher classes of task being conditional on the attainment of lower classes. If a student has not assimilated the basics then it is pointless to attempt to progress further. The implication being that tuition should be paced to match the learning ability of the student. The work of Tennyson *et al.* (1985), among others, has sought to capitalise on this realisation.

Understanding

This is distinguished from capability in that it does not refer to understanding of a particular system. It refers to an individual's understanding of the problem to be solved or the task to be undertaken.

A classic example of the effect of domain understanding on task performance was given by Chase and Simon (1973). The domain of chess was used for investigating the effects of domain knowledge on the task of replicating mid-game board positions. Subjects were either chess naive or of a very high grade. Mid-games were created from real positions or by random distribution of representative samples of chess pieces on a board. Subjects were then asked to quickly look at these mid-games for later reproduction of the mid-game. When the pieces were randomly placed the novices and masters performed similarly, but when real mid-games had to be reproduced the masters performed much better than the novices. The implication of this finding is that individuals who understand a domain can call upon cognitive structures to help in task performance.

This has major implications for applications such as expert systems, where difficulty is often experienced at the user interface with respect to the explanation facilities provided. Larkin *et al.* (1988):

"The system cannot explain its reasoning in a manner that human beings can easily understand. A major reason is that general knowledge, shared by the system and the human, cannot provide an explicit basis for explanation, but becomes submerged in a morass of specific details."

With regard to adaptive systems there is a large question mark over what can be assumed to be shared knowledge. Different users will have varying amounts of knowledge about any particular domain. Ideally explanations should be tailored to accommodate these differences. Hence users would not be overloaded with details with which they are already familiar and would not be given explanations that could not be understood due to a lack of the necessary concepts on the user's behalf, Savory (1986).

Expectations

Works such as those by Walther and O'Neill (1974) demonstrate how a user's previous experience of a particular mode of interaction creates expectations. This work categorised people as being novices, of little computer experience, or having a lot of experience. Trials were then run on either a tailorable or inflexible text editor. One of the interesting findings was that users who had both a neutral or negative attitude towards the tailorable system and minimal previous experience made more syntax errors. The authors suggest this might be explained by the users having low expectations as a result of realising that greater mental effort was required, on their part, in order to gain benefit from the tailorability of the system.

When moving from one system to another (Polson et al. 1987) users will transfer conceptual models developed during interaction with the first system. These expectations may be as simple as the naming conventions for commands.

Motives

When performing any series of tasks, users will be doing so in order to achieve some goal. They are motivated in some manner. The same sequence of tasks may be performed by different individuals or indeed by the same individual on different occasions to different ends. For instance, two people may place different requirements on a decision support system. One user may want to know what actions to take in the short-term and will require raw data. The other may wish to take long-term strategic actions that are best supported by trend information presented graphically.

In an analysis of persons ranging in job positions, Rosson (1984) found great differences in how "efficient" users were in making use of the task completion methods available to them and concludes that

> "Part of the problem is undoubtedly motivational -- in some cases, users may well suspect that some better way of accomplishing a goal exists, but simply not wish to spend the time to learn about it. This type of problem is a hard one to design away, as it is difficult to provide motivation that doesn't exist. However, designers can certainly attempt to reduce the motivational pre-requisite for extending knowledge, by making the new skills as easy and safe to learn as possible."

An alternative would be to adaptively provide advice on how to complete tasks, offering such advice in a timely fashion to those users who would appreciate it.

Requirements

This category is similar to motives, but is thought of on a shorter time scale. On a single occasion a user's requirements may be for accuracy while, on another, expediency may be of paramount importance.

Cognitive Strategies

A limited amount of empirical evidence exists for the existence of differences in cognitive strategy with regard to computer interaction. The work of Lawson (1979) demonstrated a distinct dichotomy between architects and designers when attempting to solve "block" problems. The architects were very solution oriented while the scientists tended to be problem oriented, trying to understand a path to the solution.

The implication of such a finding is that different strategies should be supported. At a high level the individual difference is the user's professional training and has import for the design of computer aided design tools. It is easy to see that the lower level difference of focusing on the problem or solution may have import in other applications such as decision support systems. Some users may wish to perform scenario generation while others would be more at ease with problem modelling tools as an aid to decision making. The latter would presumably expend more effort attempting to comprehend the dynamics of the problem and the reasons why a scenario might occur.

Cognitive Abilities

The psychology literature abounds with empirical evidence for different types of memory and attention mechanisms. For instance, the distinction between semantic and episodic memory proposed by Tulving (1972). This dichotomy is maintained in the user modelling component of the UNIX Consultant system (Wilensky *et al.* 1984) to predict user input and adapt output to meet user needs.

Egan and Gomez (1982) performed a correlational study between a number of abilities and performance in learning to use a text editor. Psychometric tests were used to assess users' abilities to make semantic associations, remember spatial arrangements and general reading skill. The results showed a strong correlation between spatial memory abilities and text editing performance, particularly with what might be called "navigational errors". Different editors place lesser or greater requirements on spatial memory. The implication for adaptive systems are that, where spatial memory can be assessed then editors be provided that take account of individual user's abilities.

Preferences

Just as individuals display expectations on the basis of previous experience of computer systems, individuals may also have preferences due to non-computer experiences. For instance, some may prefer computer driven dialogues as opposed to user driven ones. Gargan *et al.* (1988) took a rule-based approach to providing an adaptive interface responsive to individual preferences. Users were modelled with regard to their preferences to modality redundancy. These models then affected the mode of presenting information, that is whether it be presented for perception as a visual, auditory or tactile signal.

Holynski *et al.* (1988) built an Adaptive Graphics Analyser (AGA), that interactively adapts screen images to meet user's requirements. This was achieved by having users rate images, generated by the

AGA, on a five point scale of likeability. Each image had a number of associated variables including balance, busyness, complexity, regularity and symmetry. Following this a preference evaluation module attempted to use the ratings and image variability data to generate further images that the user would rate as attractive. Initial findings are encouraging and the authors suggest that the work may lead to the building of systems that can select the most popular way to display particular images or even animated images for specified products and populations of user.

Temporal Changes

This slot crosses all of the other categories, in that for any individual changes will take place over time. Experience can only be gained over time and, in turn, leads to alterations in abilities, comprehension, expectations, etc.

One of the main findings of a study by Maskery (1984) was that frequency of use was a major determinant of a subject's capability. Subjects were given an adaptive user interface to a set of statistical and graph-plotting tools. Subjects who used the tools at consistent intervals rather than at irregular intervals showed better performance, more acceptance of errors and faster refamiliarisation times. In addition, dispersed usage seemed to render subjects more cognizant of and accepting of the system's adaptive behaviour. Such findings have implications for the introduction of users to adaptive systems and the types of application for which adaptation might be advantageous. The experiment also found a significant decrease in user capability after a break of some weeks away from the system. This strongly suggests a possibility for systems to model users' exposure to a system as a basis for inferring possible changes in capability.

The above list, generated by the AID project, does not contain any specific personality traits such as introversion/extraversion or "negative fear of failure". These were excluded on the basis that it will be impossible to identify personality factors directly from users and difficult to infer them from user interaction sequences. The system would therefore have to engage the user in some kind of pre-test in order to assess their personality traits. This would be both time consuming and intrusive. Basically, it is our strong belief that personality factors cannot be the triggers for adaptation on pragmatic grounds.

Situation Specificity

Many candidate individual differences (ID) exist as exemplified above. For any single system, it is unlikely that each ID will be of equal importance.

This point can be made most clearly through examples. Taking the simple example of an automatic teller machine (ATM) versus an expert system, striking differences will exist in the user populations taken as a whole. In the case of the ATM, the user population will be very diverse but the task relatively straightforward. Thus individual differences on a cognitive strategy or motive dimension are unlikely to be of much consequence. For an expert system, the case is likely to be quite different. If the system does not mirror the cognitive strategies and motives of distinct users, then it is likely to be met with scepticism and disenchantment. For instance, expert system users are usually motivated by either a need for diagnostic decision support or a need to be educated. Users would be dissatisfied with such systems if they appeared to be lecturing when diagnostic analysis was required and vice versa. For the ATM, differences in motor skills or even the static characteristics of anthropometry must be catered for while these will be of little consequence in the case of an expert system user.

The impact of temporal changes will also be quite different depending on the application. Short term changes to an individual's characteristics are unlikely to be a viable basis on which to adapt where a system is used for short durations or infrequently. By the time the adaptations have taken place the user would probably have stopped interacting with the system and there would be no positive transfer effect to the user's next interaction with the system.

Highly complex tasks, by definition, require more mental work on the part of the user. Performance on such tasks are most likely to be impacted by differences in cognitive functioning. Similarly the utility of educational packages is likely to be most impacted by the user's ability to learn and how this is reflected in the operation of the package.

The point being made is that for any one application where the provision of adaptive features are being considered there will not be a need to consider every possible dimension of variability. In fact the utility of any adaptive feature will be signified in the user variability analysis conducted during application specification.

PURPOSE of Adaptive Systems

Zadeh (1963) in characterising adaptive behaviour, stated that "our premise is that all systems are adaptive, and that the real question is what they are adaptive to, and to what extent". The previous sections discussed those aspects of a system's environment, specifically dimensions of the system's users to which that system might be adapted or to which they may become adapted. This section addresses the question of extent of adaptedness. To again quote Zadeh, "every system is adaptive with respect to some set of sources or performance criterion".

Such performance criteria are often set for computer systems. Criteria for reliability and maintainability are commonplace in contracts between client and vendor. Similarly it is becoming more common for interactive systems to be assessed against usability criteria; with over-performing being a bonus for the client. With regard to adaptive systems it is important to establish whether the adaptive features *per se* produce an improvement in performance under prevailing environmental conditions. That is with respect to users and the tasks they are trying to perform. The evaluation of benefits accruing will be addressed fully in Chapter 6.

The procurement or production of any system occurs due to some perceived need or benefit. Explicit objectives will have to be met if the operational system is to be deemed a success against the original case for its production. Of course examples do exist of systems satisfying needs not envisaged originally and reaching objectives that had not been considered. The Renault 5 car was to be a market filler until other models were ready to be marketed. Its popularity resulted in it establishing itself to such an extent that it would not have been good business to withdraw it.

The primary objective or purpose in building adaptive user interfaces is quite clear: to improve human-computer interaction. Unfortunately, when taking individual examples of adaptive interfaces, it does not suffice to speak of "improvements in interaction". Even during the conceptualisation of an adaptive system, it is necessary to keep in mind an answer to the all pervasive question, "why bother?". What are the actual improvements that are going to accrue from the effort invested in its production? On what basis are we going to quantify interaction with the system in order to establish the value or even validity of the adaptive feature?

Thus, it is necessary to establish the purpose, for the investment in building any adaptive system. To this end, a list of potential purposes has been generated. Knowing the "purpose" helps to keep one's "eye on the ball". It is all too easy to get side-tracked by the architectural or physical elegance of a solution and lose sight of the problem. This can lead to the production of sophisticated solutions, but to the wrong problem. The list of purposes discussed below are certainly not definitive and may surprise because of their generality. However, it is important to frame the potential of a technological advantage with respect to the areas where it will provide leverage - to indicate its applicability.

Extend Systems Lifespan

The system is designed and implemented in such a manner as to achieve longevity in the marketplace. A favourite engineering term is "design for maintainability", which recognises that changes will occur in a system's environment. If a system can "react" to these changes, either automatically, semi-automatically or by external intervention, then its life expectancy will be greater. Of course, longevity also comes from being well adapted at birth.

Widen System's User Base

The market for computer systems is growing very quickly. Computer technology is diversifying into new markets and being offered to an ever increasing population. No longer is it the case that senior management and data processing departments are the major users. Point of sale systems and warehouse management systems are just two examples where information technology is increasingly being used by blue collar workers. This diversification strongly suggests a need for a new approach to user interfacing that acknowledges the heterogeneity of end-users in the dimensions previously discussed.

Adaptive interfacing techniques are one technique for providing technology that has utility to a greater diversity of users than previously possible.

Enable User Goals

Enabling users to achieve their objectives is exactly why computer technology exists, but it is all too often the case that a single system will not enable persons to achieve their goals in the manner they wish. All too often retrospective analysis of a system's use will demonstrate under-utilisation of a system's functionality by end-users. Nickerson (1981) found that users usually chose to use the functionality of a system with which they were presently familiar. In so doing they never became familiar with many of a system's facilities. Jerrams Smith (1985) provides many examples of how UNIX users achieve their goals by suboptimal means. There seems to be a disposition among some users to continue performing tasks by tried and tested means rather than realising more efficient mechanisms for achieving their aims.

Enabling user goals is a highly desirable objective to be met by any system. Given the likely reasons for users failing to attain their objectives, the provision of adaptive interfaces for this purpose is desirable.

Satisfy User Wants

Technologists sensitive to human qualities strive to ensure that end-users will be satisfied with the tools and systems they are expected to use. The belief being that where working conditions are satisfying, less absenteeism and higher productivity will result. With information technology in particular, there is always a worry of producing a feeling of alienation within the workforce. A lot of technology is still viewed with scepticism and resistance because of beliefs that it will reduce manning levels and de-skill jobs (Kemp and Clegg, 1987; Wilkinson, 1983). In addition, during interaction with the technology, users may get frustrated by a system's lack of flexibility and insistence on conciseness and specificity. Workers often imbue systems with abilities they most certainly do not possess, anthropomorphising them with properties such as intelligence and even second sight. At a gross level, such users are displacing inabilities or lack of knowledge onto the system and are voicing disfavour at the system's insistence that they meet its strict requirements. Because this sort of disfavour is so commonplace, providing adaptive interfaces that acknowledge individuality and attempt to adapt to the user is desirable. The hoped-for result being increased subjective satisfaction and acceptance of the system.

Improve Operational Accuracy

In some circumstances, the primary objective of making enhancements to an existing system will be to improve its operational accuracy. This does not refer to the accuracy of functions performed by the system but to the accuracy of communication between human and system, and the accuracy of human and system together in performing some task. For instance, the accuracy of producing a printable copy or the tracking of targets on a display. Accuracy of operation is one of the most tangible usability measures (Shackel, 1986) that can be ascribed to a system. If accuracy can be improved through adaptive mechanisms as seems feasible, then this becomes a reasonable purpose for an adaptive system.

Increase Operational Speed

Productivity on any task may be improved by enhancing the speed of interaction. The "may be" qualification is necessary because increased speed often leads to reduced accuracy. Nevertheless, where speed is deemed important, adaptive mechanisms might be employed to achieve this objective.

Reduce Operational Learning

Before productive work can be accomplished, there is always a period during which the user will need to learn how to use the system in order to be able to accomplish objectives. This operational learning time can often be quite expensive requiring an investment in training and an acceptance that a period of poor productivity will exist. Following initial training, a further time of consolidation and secondary learning will take place during which optimal working will not be achieved. In addition, periods away from the system may necessitate some relearning. Adaptive mechanisms may be suitably employed to reduce such training requirements, and thus reduce overheads associated with the introduction of information technology. This is not to say that such reductions would lessen the user's understanding of the technology, only that their speed of learning of the system would be improved. On-line training packages are an example of a non-adaptive means provided for just this purpose.

Enhance User Understanding

The primary purpose of Computer Aided Learning packages is one of enhancing user understanding, but here we are referring to the provision of features that will enhance a user's comprehension of the particular system being used. While many computer users may be able to perform adequately on the basis of task-specific knowledge, advantages can be obtained by having generalisable understanding of the system. For instance, when a novel situation arises the user who only knows the commands and parameters to type in order to open and delete files, will not be as well informed as the user who knows rules for combining commands and parameters. The point is that users can benefit from knowing how a system operates - at a suitable level of abstraction - and not just how to perform specific tasks. It is feasible to provide adaptive features that can enhance user understanding of a system and thus render them more capable of dealing with novel situations through generalisation of principles.

The above list of purposes for providing an adaptive user interface is not definitive and it is somewhat general. Nonetheless, it has been found to be useful, lest we forget why we are producing a particular adaptive feature or system. A number of points need to be made regarding use of the list. Firstly, although an adaptive feature can be provided with a particular purpose in mind, the side-effects this may have on other purposes should not be forgotten. For instance, the trade-off between speed and accuracy of operation is easily forgotten as is the trade-off between reducing operational learning and increasing operational understanding. The methodology developed for the project, and described later, helps to avoid some of these difficulties, particularly through documenting testable assumptions at an early stage of system design.

However it may also be the case that a particular adaptive system is employed to meet two or more purposes and that these purposes are hierarchically related. For instance, increasing operational accuracy may be seen as a means to achieving subjective satisfaction. Indeed, when taking individual examples of adaptive systems, finer grain purposes are likely to be identified than those listed above. An example of this might be adaptive defaulting or second guessing of user input in the hope that this decreases the number of required keystrokes. Reduced keystroking of itself has little value, it is the effect this has on operational speed which is actually important and this would be the actual purpose of providing adaptive defaulting.

USER INTERFACE DYNAMICS

Given that sufficient user variability exists to warrant the provision of adaptive mechanisms and that a purpose or purposes with sufficient foreseeable benefits can be established, the next question is how? How can or should the user interface adapt on the basis of user variability in order to achieve its purpose?

The potential for flexibility and the need for it at the user interface is often reflected in the guidelines that authors produce with regard to the design of "user-friendly" interfaces. As pointed out by Maguire (1982), these guidelines often conflict, the reason being that they have been generated on the basis of work in a specific application area or with a group of users who are not representative of a wider population. By taking some of these guidelines both user differences, purposes and user interface dynamics can be identified.

Help

This refers to user initiated requests for assistance. Help is often provided on-line at one of a number of levels of detail. For instance, it may provide the user with information about the effects of particular commands or a list of commands that can be used given the present state of the dialogue. The prime objectives of "help" facilities is one of enabling the user to continue with their task. If they get into difficulties then help is available. It will not affect their present task or the state of the system but it may provide sufficient assistance such that further progress can be made. Cohill and Williges (1982) state

"... for novice software system users, the optimum HELP system configuration was one in which the user controls the initiation and selection of HELP displays, and the information is stored in hard-copy manuals."

What is interesting in this statement, when considering adaptive systems, is that it is qualified by the predicate "novice users". The authors are not suggesting that all users be given the same sort of HELP facility. Similarly, Morland (1983) states

> "At the first occurrence of an error, a very brief diagnostic would signal the user and give him a clue to the nature of the fault. Then if the error is repeated or if the user fails to understand the first message, a more extensive explanation would be presented to assist the novice user in correcting the problem. Finally, if the user is still uncertain as to the correct response, he would be able to explicitly summon assistance ..."

In this statement, provision of a number of levels of help is being advocated with a dependency on the user's understanding as to whether the dialogue continue or not. Roemer and Chapanis (1982), suggested that the reading level of help messages might also effect learning performance and user attitudes. They proposed using the "fog index" (Gunning, 1959) to pitch help messages at an appropriate reading level for users.

In these few pieces of work it can be seen that designers have flexibility over the method of presentation of help messages, the wording of help messages and how much control resides with the user. This flexibility being mediated by the attributes of the end-user.

Windowing and Scrolling

There are a variety of dialogue styles to choose between. Rather than scrolling command based screens, there now exists the possibility of Windows, Icons, Mice and Pop-up Menus (WIMP), What You See Is What You Get (WYSIWYG) and Direct Manipulation type interfaces to name a few. In comparing user preferences towards windowing and scrolling, Bury *et al.* (1982) found appreciable differences between users:

> "Although the majority of the novice users tested defined the system to window, a fair number of users (12% with the diamond-

shaped layout, and 30% with the square layout), did define the system to scroll."

This work demonstrates how user differences, in terms of preferences, should be accommodated. The recommendation is that the choice remain with the user. Taking this one step further the user could be modelled such that, across applications, their preferences were automatically pandered to by the system.

Command Language

Every interactive system has a command language whether it be communicated explicitly as text, chosen from menus or indicated by sequences of function keys. The choice of names for commands can also be quite variable. Dumais and Landauer (1982),

"... experienced typists who are computer novices do not use the same language as system designers do to describe text-editing operations. And, for the most part, they don't even agree with each other. Thus one person's obvious command names may not be another's."

The implication of this for adaptive systems is that the command language of the system accommodate these differences between users. This is supported by the work of Thomas and Schneider (1984) who state:

"Use the terminology of the user. This implies spending some time finding out what that terminology is. It does not imply avoiding all technical terms."

The work of Barnard *et al.* (1982) is also worth noting. To quote:

"The potential influences of alternative command names could be pursued more profitably if the kind of demands imposed by particular names are analysed in conjunction with broader task demands as well as the cognitive predispositions of the potential user population."

Thus the choice of command language, or more specifically the flexibility that might be supported by an adaptive system, appears to be mediated by user's previous experience, specific task demands and cognitive dispositions. Opportunity for adaptive control of command languages exists and could be fruitfully capitalised upon to improve the user interface of interactive systems.

Error Messages

The commonest type of error message is one that attempts to convey to the user that their input cannot be understood. Some systems attempt to be more helpful by indicating a possible source for the error or a possible means of proceeding.

The objective of having such messages is simply that of identifying an inaccuracy by the user or an inability on the part of the system. Nowadays, most error messages attempt to identify the source of the error in the user's input, thus aiding them in recasting their input. As with other user interface components, the literature affords recommendations as to how error messages can best be provided. Schneiderman (1979), makes the following statements:

"In designing a system for novices, every attempt should be made to make the user at ease, without being patronizing or too obvious."

"Constructive messages and positive reinforcement produce faster learning and increase user acceptance."

While Schneiderman is not advocating the use of adaptive techniques, the statements do suggest that much design flexibility exists with regard to the provision of error messages even to the extent that they can be ascribed human characteristics. In addition, design can affect learning and acceptance by the user. The ever pervasive catchall phrase, "novice" is used as a caveat to such recommendations, suggesting that individual differences need to be taken into consideration.

By considering a few of the available guidelines for a few of the user interface attributes that could be adapted within a system, a feeling can be gained for the range of flexibility that could be used to accommodate diverse user populations. Space does not permit consideration of such attributes as "prompts", "format", "input devices", etc. The point is that for any particular application many design variants are possible and decisions should be mediated by recognition of user and task variability. A method for making well founded design decisions is what is required.

METRICS

The project has developed a set of metrics to make explicit the basis for differentiating system performance for users and to represent the categories of data that have been found to be essential elements of an adaptive system (Browne, Trevellyan, Totterdell and Norman, 1987). The metrics have been found useful in providing a framework for the design, building and evaluation of adaptive systems. Specifying the metrics at an early stage in the design process aided the project in clarifying the objectives and rationale behind proposed systems. Additionally the metrics guided the evaluation of specific systems and provided the means by which the findings could be generalised. Six categories of metrics were identified:

Objective Metric (Obj. M.)

This states the objective of the adaptive system. For example, the objective may be to speed the user's interaction with the system, or to decrease a user's error rate, or to increase user satisfaction. Many of the objectives for an adaptive system will be from the list of purposes. If the objective is for example to increase interaction speed then consideration of the metric during design should highlight the need to include in the system some means of measuring and recording user response times.

Theory Assessment Metric (Tass. M.)

The theory assessment metric is required when the success of the system in obtaining its objective is related only indirectly to the aspect of the user interaction that the system is attempting to improve. The means for attaining the objective may rest on an untested theory.

For example, adaptation could be based on a theory that attempts to decrease error rates in order to increase user satisfaction. In order to test this theory it is essential that the system collects data on error rates; even though this does not reflect the objective of the whole system. In this case error rates are the theory assessment metric.

Trigger Metric (Trig. M.)

The trigger metric describes the aspect of user interaction on which the adaptation is based, i.e. the interpreted input. The triggers for adaptation could include the latency of a user's response, keystroke sequences, error types, etc. The triggers determine what types of data must be captured by the system and form the sources for the adaptive mechanism. Triggers may be derived from the same data elements in different ways and it is essential therefore that the designer describe not only what data is captured but also how it is interpreted; for example, frequency of specific errors versus total number of errors.

Recommendation Metric (Rec. M.)

The recommendation metric provides a description of the output of the theory based part of the system. For instance, if the system's recommendation at any point in the interaction is to increase the help given to a user then this recommendation should be captured. This is essential so that the effects of recommendations can be related to user interaction behaviour.

Generality Metric (Gen. M.)

The generality metric provides an assessment of the range of applicability of the adaptive system both in terms of the user population and in the range of tasks to which the system will apply. This metric provides a basis for establishing the scope of performance for which the system is valid. Examples of the generality metric might be the assumed expertise of the user or the size of the application command set. The generality metric should also describe the unknowns - those variables which, it is believed, may affect performance but about which data is currently not available.

Implementation Metric (Imp. M.)

The implementation metric assesses whether there are aspects of the implementation of the adaptive system which have a detrimental effect on the performance of the system. The extra processing required by the introduction of adaptation may slow down the system response to the extent that the benefits of providing adaptation are outweighed.

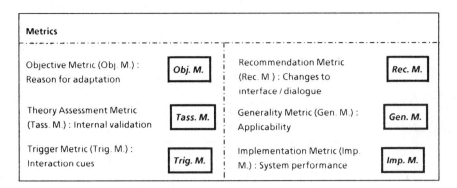

Fig. 2.1 Metrics for adaptive systems.

The various metrics make explicit the design information which is essential for the operation of an adaptive system and establishes the feasibility of the approach. The pervasive nature of this approach should not be underestimated. It provides a unifying framework for the justification, design, construction and evaluation of adaptive systems, and could equally be applied to conventional systems. In this regard it provides the means for a direct mapping between the structure of the design and the implemented system, with all the benefits that that brings (Moran, 1983).

Figure 2.2 shows the logical components of an adaptor, which is the intermediary between the user interface and the application software. It also shows where the metrics apply in relation to the components of an adaptive system. Data from user interaction which forms the basis for adaptations are described as Trig. M. The theory that determines Tass. M. is the relationship between the data in the models and the effect that changes have on the user interface. Tass. M. is also captured from monitoring user interaction with the system in those cases where the system can only assess the effect of these changes indirectly. Thus Trig. M. and possibly Tass. M. are the data that the user and/or task model are based on. The changes to the interface are described using Rec. M. If the purpose or objective of the adaptations can be assessed on-line then Obj. M. is also monitored directly from the interaction. Gen. M., the applicabilty of the adaptations across tasks is usually measured off-line, not during interaction. Imp. M. is generally measured off-line, although aspects of Imp. M. could be automatically gathered, for instance, speed of operation.

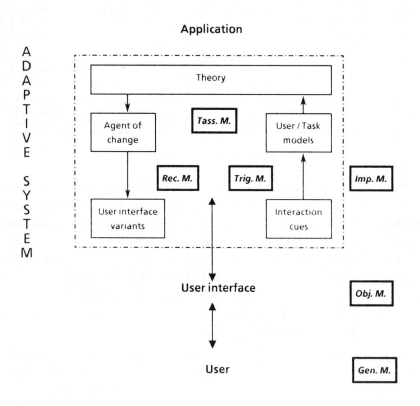

Fig. 2.2 Application of metrics.

METHODOLOGY FOR DESIGN

Many current design methodologies are very rigid, encouraging the designer to arrive at a single specification for the system and interaction with users. In contrast, in the design of an adaptive system, it is necessary to employ an approach which allows the designer to identify and cater for variability where it arises. The original work on the project (Clowes, 1988) gave rise to a simple design tool - Methodology for Adaptive Interface Design (MAID) - which permitted a staged approach to data gathering for design of adaptive features in systems. This was later transformed from a paper based method to the 'Deferred Design Tool' (DDT),

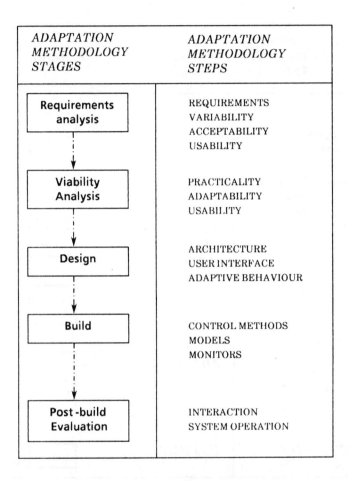

ADAPTATION METHODOLOGY STAGES	ADAPTATION METHODOLOGY STEPS
Requirements analysis	REQUIREMENTS VARIABILITY ACCEPTABILITY USABILITY
Viability Analysis	PRACTICALITY ADAPTABILITY USABILITY
Design	ARCHITECTURE USER INTERFACE ADAPTIVE BEHAVIOUR
Build	CONTROL METHODS MODELS MONITORS
Post-build Evaluation	INTERACTION SYSTEM OPERATION

Fig. 2.3 The design process for adaptive systems.

The stages in the methodology are shown in Fig. 2.3 . The method was based on the introduction of additional steps in the design process, which in conjunction with the identification of metrics provides an approach to identifying opportunities for the use of adaptive techniques. In particular they cover the definition of : user and task requirements; potential variability; acceptability of change; practicality of implementation. The considerations taken into account and identified in the first two of these stages are shown in Fig. 2.4 below.

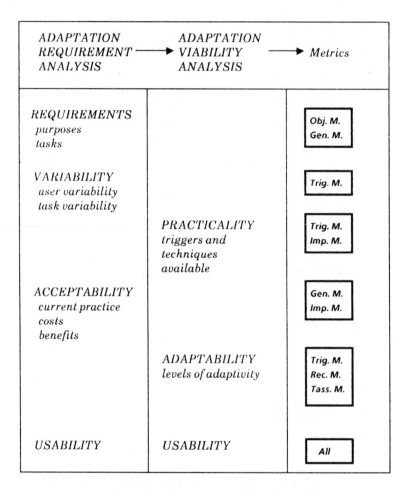

Fig. 2.4 Derivation of metrics for adaptive systems.

Requirements Analysis

At the initial development stage, the requirement for an adaptive system is addressed. By so doing irrelevant or erroneous design avenues can be dismissed at an early point, thus focusing development on the most promising areas for adaptation. The REQUIREMENTS step establishes the purpose of the system and what it is desirable to achieve. That is to establish the business or personal objectives to be met by the system. An example might be increased work throughput as in the Bloggs scenario described at the beginning of this chapter. Thus, even at the very first stage of development the objectives (Obj. M.) and the planned scope (Gen. M.) of the system can be established. It is worth noting that the general applicability of the adaptations is a desirable at this stage, and cannot be guaranteed. The second step involves an assessment of the possible VARIABILITY which may be drawn on to provide alternative design scenarios. This is accomplished by identifying measures (Trig. M.) on which user or task variability can be quantified or qualified as a basis for modelling and ultimately driving any adaptations. This step may provide further focus for the development. For instance, if personality differences were a pervasive differentiator of users but there is no opportunity to assess personality then further development in this direction would be curtailed. The third step seeks to assess ACCEPTABILITY, in terms of benefits against system costings (Imp. M.). Assuming that the requirements analysis still suggests that there is worth in developing an adaptive system the USABILITY criteria should be established. For instance, the number of errors per representative task and the average time to perform those tasks. Usability criteria are not treated in the same manner as the other design steps. This step does not define any additional metrics but makes use of the metrics that have already been identified. It has to be added that the usability criteria identified through this method do not necessarily represent the full set of criteria that may be applied to conventional systems.

Viability Analysis

The viability analysis aims to establish the relationship between the identified variability in the user population with adaptations to take place at the user interface.

The first step of this stage examines the PRACTICALITY of accomplishing a design that meets the objectives established in the requirements analysis. The principal concerns are to establish the:

- Triggers for adaptation and how they will be captured (Trig. M.).

- The changes to be made at the user interface (Rec. M.).

- The assumptions on which these adaptations will be placed (Tass. M.).

These metrics establish the theory on which the adaptations are to be based, and the inputs and outputs necessary for the execution of this theory. For instance, in the Bloggs story, the theory was that increased work throughput (Obj. M.) could be achieved by decreasing errors (Tass. M.). Also that the reduction in error rates could be achieved by adaptively changing the information content of help messages (Rec. M.). The error rates (Trig. M.) also served as the basis for modelling individuals and ultimately for triggering the adaptations.

The manner by which the trigger data (Trig. M.) are obtained whether through negotiation with the user, or by the system automatically, possibly in combination with direct assessment of the utility of the adaptations, determines the level of ADAPTABILITY of the system. Additional detailed definition of the USABILITY criteria are now possible in the light of the system's adaptiveness, amounting to a viability assessment and statement of requirements for evaluation. Although usability is becoming an accepted aspect of interactive software development methods, the basis for the criteria and the way in which they should influence design are not always self evident. Significantly, this approach provides an immediate relationship between user interface design issues and the definition and measurement of relevant criteria.

Taken together these two phases offer a feasibility assessment which seeks to exclude some design variants. Those variants that remain are specified in terms of metrics which are explicit and available for evaluation and testing throughout the remaining phases of the methodology. The effect that an early declaration of this sort has on the evaluation of systems, and the embedding of suitable data collection mechanisms as part of the design process, has led us to re-assess the traditional role of evaluation. The metrics that have been identified in the first phase of the method would then (Fig. 2.5) be employed in the following way:

Design

Having established the need for, practicality of and theory behind the adaptive system, design work can begin. The software

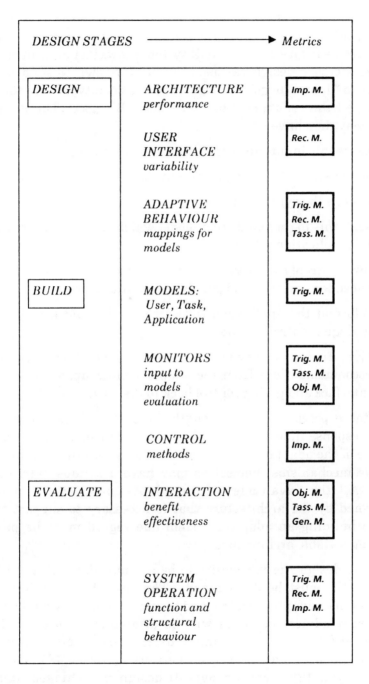

Fig. 2.5 Metrics to design, build and evaluate adaptive systems.

ARCHITECTURE of the system will need to be such that its performance (Imp. M.) does not counteract the benefits to be gained from the adaptations. Taking a scenario of providing an adaptive user interface to an electronic mail system shows just how intrusive a poor architecture design can be. The user wishes to send a mail message to "John Bloggs". The message has been typed and the user has created the command line "send John Bloggs". The adaptive system may then have to:

- parse this input into a command and parameter,

- send these as triggers to a user model,

- change the syntax of the line,

- send this to an application model which will then pass it on to the application software,

- await a reply from the application model which will have to check for syntactic and possibly semantic errors,

- reformat the application software's output and pass it to the dialogue controller, and

- the dialogue controller may then have to take recommendations from the adaptor before updating the user interface and giving control back to the user.

All of these processes can be lengthy, resulting in an inordinate system response time at the user interface. If in such a scenario the objective of the adaptations is to increase work throughput, then the adaptive mechanisms themselves may have a serious detrimental effect. All the advantages of the adaptations *per se.* may be outweighed by the architecture that is necessary to support them. Thus in building an adaptive system due regard must be paid to designing a viable architecture.

During design the variability to be accommodated at the USER INTERFACE must be determined. That is, what is going to be changed under adaptive control and to what extent. It would be easy to say that advice messages will be altered, but this would be insufficient. Only by producing a user interface design using a technique such as state transition networks (Woods, 1970) or state charts (Harel, 1988) can an overall design be achieved and the variability to be supported within this design stated. For instance, if advice messages are to be adaptively controlled, what aspect of them will adapt? Will it be their time of presentation, the format of the presentation, or their content? If the latter is the case then how will the content be adapted? Will there be "n" different advice messages each of which can take "m" different forms? Will the adaptor determine the manifestation of the advice message as an absolute, or relatively with respect to the previous invocation of an advice message. The design of the user interface must determine the range of variability and whether it is to be provided in an absolute or relative manner. This aspect of the design establishes the specifics of the Recommendation Metric (Rec. M.).

Importantly, the design stage must specify what the ADAPTIVE BEHAVIOUR of the system is to be. Given certain triggers and certain desirable changes to the user interface, mediated by user/task modelling what is the relationship between interaction and user interface modifications going to be? This was addressed in the Bloggs story by establishing the relationship between error rate and the (adaptively controlled) content of help messages. That is the relationship between triggers (Trig. M.) and recommendations (Rec. M.) was established. This is by necessity, theoretically based with relation to the objective of the adaptations, which might be monitored indirectly as the theory assessment metric (Tass. M.). For example, if a monitor identifies errors for input to a user model and this model, as a component of the adaptor, recommends the "level of help", then this relationship might be depicted as in Fig.2.6, which shows that the adaptive system will display a behaviour that gives more help to those users who make most errors. For any one adaptive system a number of adaptive behaviours might be exhibited, each of which would need to be described. At this point the expected relationship between the changes at the user interface (Rec. M.) and the objectives of the adaptations should also be described to permit subsequent evaluation of the theory (Tass. M.) on which these behaviours are based.

Build

Having designed an architecture, determined the variability of the user interface and specified the adaptive behaviour of the system it is now time to produce code for supporting and populating it. Firstly, the MODELS that the system must maintain. Depending on the

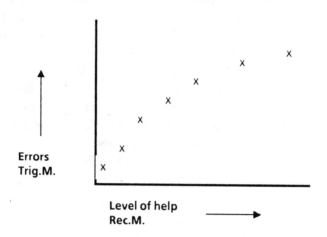

Fig. 2.6 Response of system to interaction.

findings of the REQUIREMENTS ANALYSIS, particularly the VARIABILITY step, there will be a need for a user model, a task model and possibly an application modelling component. The input to these models will be triggers (Trig. M.), that is the source of data on which adaptations are based. The models will have to maintain an up to date account of the user's present state on whichever dimensions of variability have been identified as pertinent, the task(s) they are presently performing or have had experience of before, and possibly a model of the application with regard to the tasks the user may wish to have performed. An application model might also hold historical and state information, such as how many mailboxes a user has, how many files are open, what access rights, etc.

In order to provide the input required by the models, MONITORS will have to be built. The most obvious one being an interaction monitor that identifies "interaction cues" such as errors, show interaction, task initiation, task completion, etc. All of these being potential triggers (Trig. M.). In addition, the monitors may collect data on user performance such that the adaptive system can analyse the worth of its adaptations (Tass. M., Obj. M.) or more simply collect data to support later off-line analysis.

One very difficult problem as discussed above is ensuring that the adaptive mechanisms themselves do not countermand the benefits of the adaptations. The CONTROL mechanism employed by the system must ensure that all the components; models; monitors; adaptors and application software communicate in a desirable and efficient fashion (Imp. M.).

Post-build Evaluation

Once the system has been built and is in operational use there remains the exercise of evaluating it *in situ*. This can be undertaken at at least two levels. Firstly, the effects the adaptations have on INTERACTION. That is, what are the benefits (Obj. M.) of the system to the end-users and how generally applicable (Gen. M.) are these benefits. Sometimes the benefits can be assessed directly by the system itself as in the case of error rates or speed of interaction. Other objectives like the subjective satisfaction experienced by users can only be assessed outside interaction with the adaptive system. Generality, is also important and often disregarded even when evaluating non-adaptive systems. The question to be answered is whether the adaptations have equal applicability to all users and across all tasks. For instance, the adaptations might only be worthwhile for those tasks that require much data entry, or only to users who have a typing speed below fifty words per minute. Generality is important so that the findings from building the adaptive system can be validated for subsequent work and limitations of the findings established.

Evaluation should also address the question of whether the adaptive system performed as designed. SYSTEM OPERATION evaluation determines whether the adaptive behaviour (Trig. M. + Rec. M.) of the system, as designed, was achieved, and whether any assumptions (Tass. M.) were valid. For instance, in the Trevellyan & Browne (1987) study, the adaptive behaviour described a Zipf distribution (Zipf, 1949) as shown in Fig. 2.7.

Because of the complicated nature of an adaptive system it is necessary to check by on-line evaluation whether the adaptive behaviour was actually exhibited by the final system. The validity of assumptions should also be checked by describing the relationship between the Theory assessment metrics (Tass. M.) and the Recommendation Metric (Rec. M.) For instance, in a system that is designed to speed work throughput by changing the level of help then

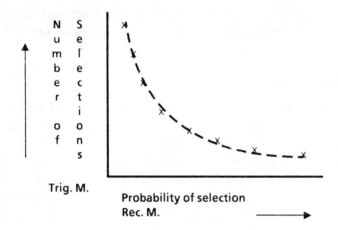

Fig. 2.7 System behaviour.

the relationship between Tass. M. and Rec. M. should describe a curve
similar to that shown in Fig. 2.8.

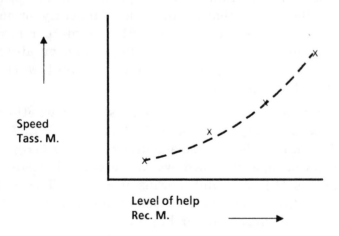

Fig. 2.8 Effect of theory on interaction.

Summary

By following the method described above the AID project has gained
substantial leverage on the problem of developing adaptive user
interfaces. Development of non-viable systems have been avoided,

better understanding of the benefits, difficulties and limitations of work has been established and a clearer conception of what constitutes an adaptive system has been afforded. In particular the adoption of the "metrics" as a framework for planning and evaluating our works has provided a basis for answering a number of questions, including:

- How will the adaptive system behave (Trig. M. + Rec. M.)?

- What effect is the theory having (Tass. M. + Rec. M.)?

- Is the adaptive system succeeding (Obj. M.)?

- What are the overheads of providing the adaptations (Imp. M.)?

- Under what circumstances are the adaptations useful (Gen. M.)?

Overall the metrics provide a way to establish the feasibility of employing adaptive techniques in the design of a system, encourage designers to identify alternative means to meet the specific needs of users in carrying out tasks and makes explicit and evaluable the basis for the final design. The method is properly viewed (Fig. 2.9) as encompassing the full range of interface design phases, integrated through the explicit declaration of the metrics for adaptive systems.

The benefits to designers of following this approach, include the:

- Highlighting of potential areas of difficulty, i.e. the need for triggers that cannot possibly be monitored.

- Identification of and hence documentation of assumptions that will exist in the system that need to be validated.

- Elucidation of the cause and effect relationship that underlies the adaptive behaviour of the system. This permits a basis for knowledgeable extension of the theoretical model embodied in the system.

- The metrics formalise the manner by which findings can be reported and as a consequence make those reports more comprehensible. In addition, they make it easier to replicate findings and relate findings to the work of others.

- Enforces consideration of how general the findings may be.

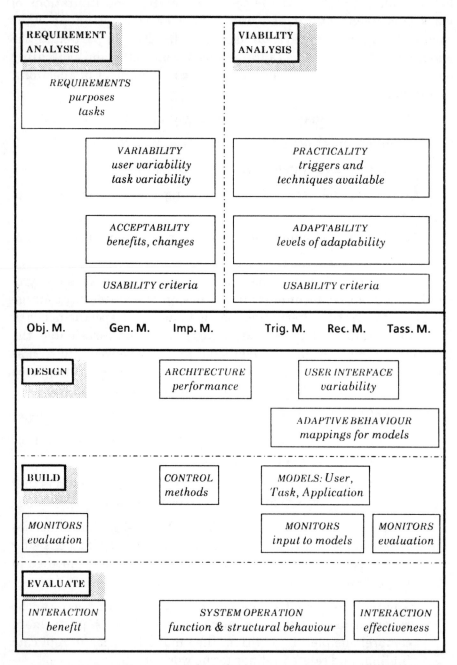

Fig. 2.9 Derivation and use of metrics - analysis and design.

CONCLUSION

It might be thought that providing an answer to the question "Is the adaptive system succeeding?" would be sufficient when performing research into adaptive systems. The inadequacy of only answering this question underpins the reasons why scientists follow rigourous design, build, evaluate procedures. Scientists of all disciplines need to understand the conditions under which something has happened (been successful) in order that they can replicate their results, generalise from their findings, and report their findings in a manner that is meaningful to fellow scientists. For these very pragmatic reasons the AID project recognised a requirement for a set of metrics and supporting method to facilitate the understanding of and reporting of findings gained from research and development of adaptive systems.

In all of this we have sought to explain the basis for selecting "adaptation" as an approach in the design of systems, and to give an account of the ways in which such designs can be justified and developed. None of this would have been possible without an underpinning view of what characterised an adaptive system and its underlying structure - an issue that we now move on to consider in some detail.

Chapter 3
Adaptation as a Problem of Design

P. Totterdell and P. Rautenbach

In this chapter we will look at some of the key theoretical issues related to the design of adaptive systems. Following an introductory section which examines the importance of the environment in the design of adaptive systems we describe a taxonomy which classifies different types of adaptive system. And in light of our views on design we examine issues relating this to a methodology for designing adaptive systems. The taxonomy has implications for the architecture of adaptive systems, and a suitable architecture is discussed. This forms the basis for describing, in later chapters, the methods to be employed in the implementation of such systems and the features of particular exemplar systems.

SYSTEMS THAT CHANGE

The standpoint taken by the AID project is that a user interface which is difficult to use is failing by not being well adapted to its users. But what do we mean by this? A good user interface should render the system usable by its users. In this sense the user interface can be thought of as something which sits between system and user and adapts the system to the user. Hence, if a user finds an interface difficult to use then the interface has not fulfilled its purpose for that user. Similarly, when circumstances change, a previously well adapted user interface may become maladapted to the new situation. This can result from the identity of the user changing (i.e. a change of user) or from the needs of the same user changing. All of these changes appear to the interface simply as user interactions and therefore the exact reason for the change may not be deducible by the system. One can debate whether a particular user sees a user interface as adaptive or simply sees it as responding appropriately to input; but what is important to a user is whether or not the interface proves to be well adapted to his or her needs despite changes in these needs and despite the same system having to serve other users with differing needs.

Two complementary views of adaptation as it relates to user interfaces have been influential in the AID project. The first is the view that the notions of adaptation and context are closely related and the second is that user interface design is a process of adapting the interface to its users and adaptive interfaces are just an extension of this process. In this chapter we take account of both these views.

THE ROLE OF THE ENVIRONMENT IN DESIGN

Adaptive systems are the means of effecting appropriate behaviour in situations that exhibit degrees of freedom, i.e. in situations that show variation along some dimension or dimensions. The measure of appropriateness is observer dependent: an external observer, a participant in the interaction, or the system itself can all assume different measures of success for the behaviour. The measures of success derive either from biological necessity or from a value-laden theory of rationality or social contract (e.g. Maynard Smith, 1986). For a situation to require an adaptive solution, one in which the parameters of the mechanism are coupled to the states of the external world, the external situation must have differentiable configurations. And in order for the adaptive mechanism to be successful it must be able to detect accurately indicators which reveal those differences which are the triggers for change.

In the case of the computer adaptive system the degrees of freedom may be found in the individual differences between users, groups of users, tasks and applications; the differences may be persistent or dynamic. The organisation of the resources available to the system shapes its modes of behaviour and determines the use to which the detection of variability is deployed. It is this response to variability with which we are principally concerned. The construction of adaptive systems is a design problem in which the designer organises a set of resources into an architecture which will behave according to a set of criteria, in the environment or environments for which it was designed. What marks out adaptive system design from the current design of computer interfaces is that with the adaptive system *the designer defers some of the design parameters such that they can be selected or fixed by features of the environment at the time of interaction.*

In fact we would wish to reverse the current perception of adaptive system design and argue that it represents not a specific but the general case for computer interface design. The current norm for interface design is to anticipate all operational circumstances by constructing systems which offer, in advance of interaction, responses that are both uniform across classes of possible conditions and unchanging. The design of adaptive systems requires the more general view that there is a range of design solutions and that the choice of design solution should be determined by the demands of the circumstances. Or to put this view another way, conventional systems are special cases of adaptive systems in which the parameters have been pre-set.

Adaptation has been applied very differently in various disciplines such as control engineering, cybernetics, biological science, psychology and computing and the systems to which the term has been applied appear to carry no more than family resemblance. The confusion is removed by recognising that the concern of adaptation is to beneficially relate a system to its environment and that the actual design configuration will be shaped by the demands of the environment.

The adaptation of a system cannot be discussed without making known the corresponding environmental objects to which it is adapted. Changes in the behaviour of a system are explainable in terms of the system's beliefs, implicit or explicit, about environmental objects. This is the case even if the objects do not have independent reality since the behaviour of the system is directed towards those objects as if they existed. This is discussed more fully in Bechtel (1985) to account for false beliefs from an intentional perspective.

For example, the initial adaptive system developed on the AID project, adjusted the *amount* of guidance it gave to a user depending on its assessment of their experience and problems. There is an implicit assumption in this system's adaptive mechanism that it is in an environment which has a varying demand for amounts of information. It is a useful design exercise to tease out these assumptions and then to compare them against the realities of the environments into which the system is actually placed. For example, it is clear that the intended environment for our adaptive system is actually made up of users requiring *qualitatively different* information rather than *different amounts* of information. The success of our system will therefore be limited by its design assumptions.

Designing computer adaptive systems means designing computing systems that fit their environment. Given the potential diversity of environments it is not surprising that the solutions are also diverse. An attempt to provide a synthetic framework of adaptive behaviour must therefore look at the very least to a functional rather than a mechanistic account because functional explanations "can explain similar outcomes produced by different means" (Staddon, 1983). Once we have identified a framework which accounts for general functional characteristics of adaptive behaviour it will then be possible to discuss design method and in later chapters to populate the general framework with specific examples.

To construct our taxonomy we make use of the Prisoner's Dilemma which was first popularised in game theory (cf. Maynard Smith, 1985). Here we present a revised version of the previously published account (Totterdell, Norman and Browne, 1987). In both accounts the framework is referred to as a taxonomy. For this we take Fleishman and Quaintances's (1984) definition of taxonomy as "the theoretical study of systematic classifications including their bases, principles, procedures and rules". The classification is of the Darwinian rather than either the Linnean or numerical type.

TAXONOMY OF ADAPTIVE SYSTEM DESIGN

The Prisoner's Dilemma is a simple game which has been used over many years by social scientists as a method for studying cooperative behaviour. In the most common version of the game there are two players and their aim is to maximise their individual gains. There are two moves in the game: C (for cooperate) and D (for defect). The players simultaneously select a move over a number of trials. One payoff matrix for the game is shown below.

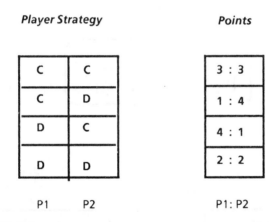

Fig. 3.1 Payoff matrix for Prisoner's Dilemma.

If both players cooperate they will receive 3 points. If they both defect they will only get 2 points. But if one defects and the other cooperates then the defector will receive 4 points and the cooperator only 1 point (Fig. 3.1). So it is to their mutual advantage to cooperate, but there is a temptation to defect.

Axelrod (1984) ran an experiment in which entrants were required to submit a computer program which played the Prisoner's Dilemma with a strategy that the entrant considered would be the most successful when played against the other entrants' programs. The programs displayed a range of different strategies. There were "Friendly" programs which were never the first to defect and "Nasty" programs which consistently defected. The most successful programs used a "Tit for Tat" strategy which started with a cooperative move and then echoed the opponent's moves. The reader is asked to consider whether the behaviour of any of these programs could be termed adaptive?

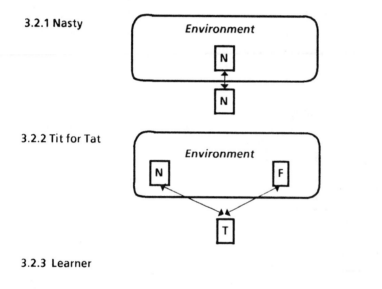

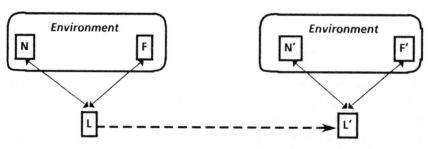

Fig. 3.2 Environments for the Prisoner's Dilemma.

One of the striking features of the programs that play the Prisoner's Dilemma is the extent to which their success is dependent on the environments that they meet. For example, if a Nasty program (N) which always defects is in an environment of similar programs (Fig. 3.2.1) then it is employing an optimal strategy; it is adapted to its environment. If the environment changes, say to include some Friendly programs (F) then the Nasty program is no longer perfectly adapted to its world and is unable to bring about the changes necessary to keep itself adapted. The Tit for Tat program (T), however, is able to vary its response to the behaviour of the programs in its environment in order to maximise its gains (Fig. 3.2.2). However, the Tit for Tat program is not learning about its environment; its behaviour is simply a "knee-jerk" response to the opponent's previous move. A simple learning program, which we shall call Learner (L), would in a changing environment have to evaluate its behaviour against the outcomes using a suitable metric (Fig. 3.2.3).

We can explore these considerations further by examining the variety of programs that could be devised for the Prisoner's Dilemma (Fig 3.3). The Nasty program is an example of a mechanism which has a single fixed response to an input stimulus (Fig. 3.3.1). The Tit for Tat program is an instance of mechanisms which possess the property of being able to both discriminate between at least two events which are perceived as having equivalent functional status and to respond differently to each event discriminated. The notion of perceived equivalent functional status is important because without it we could simply describe Tit for Tat as two mechanisms, one for each event; each no more sophisticated than the Nasty program. The Tit for Tat program recognises two types of play and responds differently to each. The generalised mechanism is shown in Fig. 3.3.2. Tit for Tat could be transformed into a learning program, Learner, by allowing it to respond with either a cooperate (C) or a defect (D) in response to a defect, and likewise in response to a cooperate, and enabling it to learn when to play each.

In fact we can distinguish two levels of functional complexity for such a program. The simpler case, shown in Fig. 3.3.3, is distinguished from a Tit for Tat mechanism by its potential to have a number of different responses to a single event. The selection of the

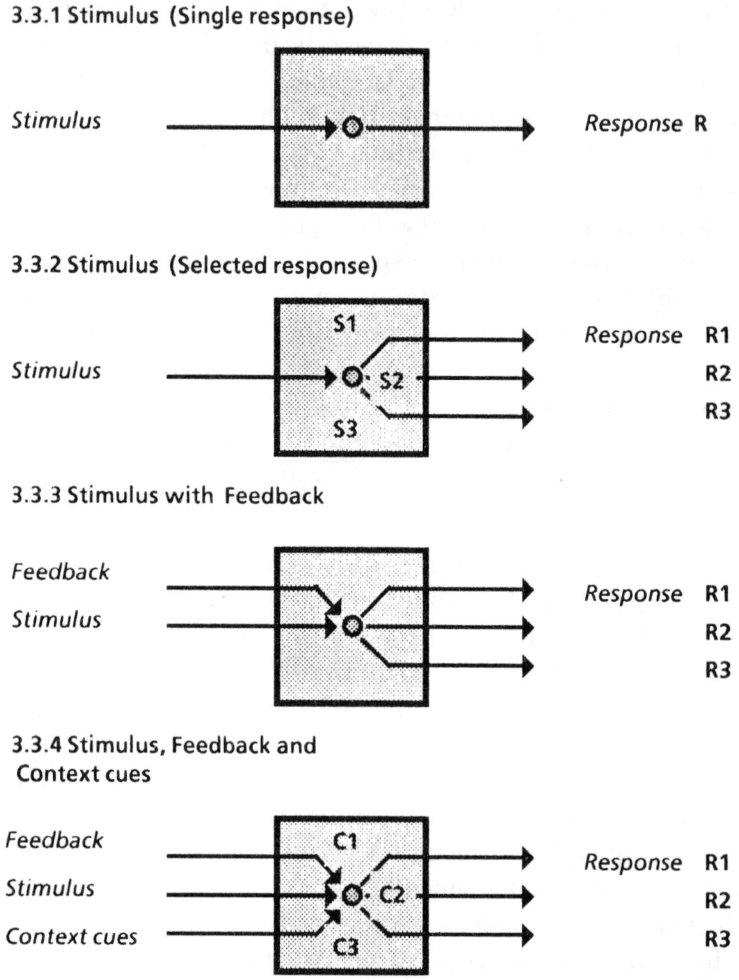

3.3.1 Stimulus (Single response)

Stimulus   Response   R

3.3.2 Stimulus (Selected response)

                  S1   Response   R1
Stimulus   S2   R2
                  S3   R3

3.3.3 Stimulus with Feedback

Feedback
Stimulus   Response   R1
                                        R2
                                        R3

3.3.4 Stimulus, Feedback and
    Context cues

Feedback   C1   Response   R1
Stimulus   C2   R2
Context cues   C3   R3

Fig. 3.3 Some mechanisms for levels of adaptivity.

response is determined by a feedback function which utilises
indicators from the environment to evaluate the effectiveness of the
response. Although the mechanism has available a number of
different responses to any single stimulus, it is unable to distinguish
between situations and hence will be no better off the next time it is

faced with the same opponent - that is it will be forced to run through its repertoire of responses to evaluate their effectiveness.

Lastly, in Fig. 3.3.4 the mechanism is able to associate cues about context, other than the primary stimulus, with particular responses. The presence or absence of these cues can then be used to both recognise future similar situations and signal particular responses - i.e. the behaviour is both learnt and context sensitive. The additional stimuli are being used to select responses for different contexts. The distinction between the primary stimulus and the context cues is a difficult one, and depends on the system's goals (or our attribution of goals). Behaviourists make a similar distinction between those stimuli which innately cue basic behaviours such as eating and drinking and those which cue behaviours through conditioning.

The two learning mechanisms we have just described test their responses on the environment. It would be useful, however, to delegate the initial evaluation to an internal function. By using an internal representation of the environment, the program would be able to predict the outcome of various courses of behaviour. It is easy to demonstrate that a program with this ability, Modeller, could have a performance advantage on the Prisoner's Dilemma. In the game shown in Fig. 3.4 Tit for Tat achieves 17 points against player 1. The arrows convey that a play has been influenced by the opponent's previous play. Instead of Tit for Tat we now use a program which evaluates the effects that the program itself can have on the environment. If the program determines that it cannot affect the moves of player 1 then it defects consistently and thereby achieves 18 points. But if it finds that it can encourage player 1 to cooperate then it might be able to achieve 22 points as shown in Fig. 3.4 .

An effective Modeller program would not be easy to build because it would require a representation of: the game and its payoffs, opponents, and metrics for success. It would take some time for the program to determine whether or not it could influence its opponents. In a restricted game such as the Prisoner's Dilemma a sophisticated strategy such as Modeller may not payoff. Although there is a lot of evidence (cf. Axelrod, 1984) to suggest that Tit for Tat is optimal for the Prisoner's Dilemma, the important point is that in some

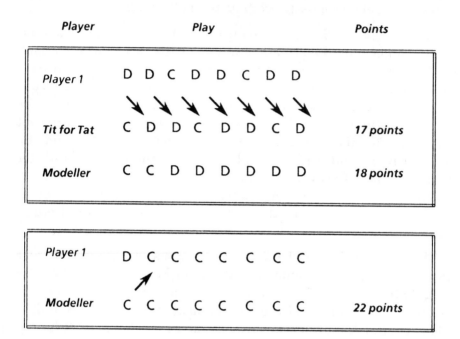

Fig. 3.4 Playing the Prisoner's Dilemma.

circumstances a system can facilitate its purposes by modelling the effects that it can have on the environment.

Finally we can ask, what would happen if the rules of the game were changed? None of the programs that we have looked at will continue to behave appropriately because they are adapted to a world which no longer exists. However, a program, Introspector, which had the ability to reorganise its internal resources in response to the changes would be able to keep the program adapted in relation to its environment with respect to the program's purposes. Such a self-modifying program would reason about its environment and change its internal rules accordingly. But if the rules of the game never change then there is no requirement for a program that can alter its domain rules. Equally, for any system it is usually possible to identify an environment which is sufficiently novel that it is unable to adapt. In particular we look for circumstances which violate the behavioural constraints determined by the "hard wiring" of the system. That is, the adaptive capability of the system is bounded.

As our programs for the Prisoner's Dilemma become more sophisticated they may incur what Staddon (1983) refers to as a "growing bookkeeping cost". The benefits gained in making the transition to the next level may not be cost effective because "it is sometimes better to be dumb and fast than intelligent and slow". Different programs will exhibit different computational complexities with respect to a problem; this defines the limits by which a system can make sense of its environment and shall be referred to as the sufficiency of a system. Every adaptive system has its own sufficiency conditions which limit the sophistication with which it can solve different problems. As the system tries to cope with a problem or environment beyond its potential its performance will degrade. The limitations of the system are revealed when we identify the environmental conditions under which the system's response is no longer rational. This is the technique Dennett (1978) uses to unmask the seemingly intelligent behaviour of the sphex wasp. The sphex wasp normally drags a cricket to the edge of its burrow, then enters and re-emerges from the burrow before dragging the cricket inside. But if the cricket is displaced slightly from its original position then the wasp will endlessly repeat the whole routine, but without locating the cricket.

Commonly, a system (or animal) will implement a simple yet effective strategy without being able to derive the effectiveness of the strategy for itself. For example, in the Prisoner's Dilemma, Tit for Tat is an optimal implementation and yet the program does not synthesise its behaviour from analysis, it is a fortuitous implementation. Sometimes, however, it is more efficient to allocate design resources to enable a system to learn through experience; more efficient not only for the designer but also for the system which would otherwise have to store the full results of a formal analysis carried out by the designer. In such cases we necessarily raise the sufficiency of the system by enabling it to learn through experience.

BIOLOGICAL PARALLELS

We believe that there are strong parallels between the levels of adaptivity we have described and the evolution of adaptive mechanisms in biological systems. In his comprehensive study of adaptive behaviour in animals, Staddon (1983) makes a distinction between innate and learned adaptation and elects to concentrate on "the ways that individual history determines behaviour". That is he is primarily interested in situations in which the environment has part responsibility for the selection of behaviour. Of the programs which we have described for the Prisoner's Dilemma only the Nasty and Friendly programs, which have a fixed pre-determined response, are innately adapted.

At the next level where we met Tit for Tat, we have a comparison with reflex mechanisms in animals. Staddon describes reflexes as depending "only on events in the present or the immediate past" and "they occur in response to an eliciting stimulus and are not readily modified by their consequences: they are almost independent of feedback". When we come on to mechanisms which use feedback, Staddon distinguishes two types of biological system which use either unsystematic variation, as in the kinetic behaviour of bacteria, or systematic variation, as in the taxic responses of animals where behaviour depends on contextual variables.

Selfridge (1984) has described the "run and twiddle" locomotive behaviour of the bacterium *Escherichia Coli* as an adaptive behavioural primitive. *E. Coli* "runs" in one direction before reversing its flagellum causing it to "twiddle" on the spot and take off in another direction. However, it will run for longer in one direction if the concentration of nutrients in the environment increases. Selfridge summarises this as an instance of the adaptive principle "if things are getting better don't change what you're doing". Run and twiddle is a fixed behaviour which is fully determined by the concentration of nutrients in the environment, i.e. it is not consequent on the history of the organism, and although it is employing feedback it is not learning in the operant sense.

Run and twiddle is an example of what biologists refer to as a fixed action pattern (FAP). A FAP is a coordinated sequence of responses cued by environmental stimulation. Once a FAP is initiated it runs off without further dependence on anything but taxic stimuli. A sign stimulus is that part of the environment that elicits the FAP. Organisms possess behavioural repertoires that contain FAPs, each one adapted to particular environmental conditions. This mechanism causes very little behavioural change to occur as a result of experience. Hence, the behaviour of *E. Coli* is "hard wired" into the design of the organism.

Dennett (1978) points out the advantage that "soft wiring" can confer on an animal. The 'soft wired' animal has a number of possible responses to a given stimulus. A particular response is reinforced and is more likely to be repeated if it is rewarded by a positive environmental effect; this is Thorndike's Law of Effect. This is the basis for operant learning in which the animal uses non-hedonic stimuli to signal reward and associates the non-hedonic stimuli with responses which are effective in bringing about the rewards.

Hetteman (1979) describes three adaptive categories for biological systems: morphology, physiology and behaviour. Morphology defines the environments in which a species can survive. Physiology allows the organism to adjust to fluctuations in the environment. And behaviour allows the organism to actively seek and transform aspects of the environment into something biologically useful. Two types of transformation are distinguished: those which rely on species-specific behaviour, and those which require the capacity to connect existing elements of behaviour with new stimulus environments (this is also referred to as psychological adaptation).

The latter transformation serves to widen the range of environments within which the individual can act. Fullan and Loubser (1972) describe the process as essentially a problem-solving activity in which the individual examines their behavioural repertoire to select the most appropriate response. This is the type of activity which we envisaged for the Modeller and Introspector programs. An interesting point that Hetteman makes about psychological adaptation is that it is an individual (or personality) concept and not a species concept. It has survival value in threatening, novel or changing environments and in more familiar environments it leads to an increase in flexibility and efficiency of behaviour.

There are many other biological comparisons that could be drawn but we will end this section with one taken from Staddon (1983) which nicely illustrates the increasing cost of moving up the levels of adaptivity. The pond animal *Stentor* has four different avoidance responses to a noxious substance: turning away, ciliary reversal, contraction into tube, and swimming away. The four responses are selected temporally; each successive response being more costly in terms of energy and interference with feeding than the preceding response but also more likely to be effective. It is also interesting to note that reintroducing the substance with all other conditions left unchanged causes *Stentor* to run through the whole program of responses again, i.e. it is unable to detect and use context.

CLASSIFICATION OF SYSTEMS

The examples from the Prisoner's Dilemma are particularly powerful in identifying the various forms of adaptive system that can be contemplated, and these categories are reinforced by consideration of the biological paradigm. Relating these considerations to computing systems provides a taxonomy of adaptive systems (Fig. 3.5), classified by levels of adaptivity. Also shown on the taxonomy are features which distinguish these levels and the functional (or design) requirements of a system at each level. This is in recognition of the fact that there will be a range of possible physical mechanisms which will satisfy a given set of design requirements at each level.

It is also true that a range of designs can satisfy the same intentional explanation (Pylyshyn, 1984). The levels could be described in terms of the intentional relationship between system and environment; but this awaits a suitable vocabulary which identifies persistent and stable intentional categories. It should be noted that there is a change in locus of intention as we move through the levels: from designer to system.

A theme which runs through all the levels is concerned with the amount of control that a system has in negotiating change. At the lowest levels the user is simply able to switch the system between different states whereas at the higher and more complex levels the system is expected to exert more intelligence in negotiating change. As we move up levels, systems appear to take on more responsibility for their behaviour. But it is important not to confuse this with the idea that the systems are taking control away from the user. In order for a higher level system to remain well adapted it requires capacities for negotiation which includes knowing when and when not to consult the user.

Prisoner's Dilemma	Evolution	*Features*	Computer Systems	
Nasty/ Friendly	Natural selection	*Selection by external agent*	Designed systems	
Player selects from range of strategies	Genetic engineering	*Deferred selection*	Adaptable/ tailorable	
Tit for Tat	Tropism/ reflexes	*Apparent learning (i.e. fully determined by design); discrimination*	Adaptive	L e v e l s
Learner	Operant conditioning	*Learning; varied responses selected for different situations; evaluation by trial and error*	Self-regulating	
Modeller	Internal evaluation	*Planning; problem solving; rule mediated representation; initial evaluation internal to the system*	Self-mediating	
Introspector	Abstraction	*Evaluating the evaluation; generalisation; meta-knowledge*	Self-modifying	

Fig. 3.5 Taxonomy of adaptive systems.

It is possible to take particular instances of existing computer adaptive systems and classify them within our taxonomy (Fig. 3.6). This classification distinguishes between different forms of adaptive system and indicates the potential for additional and more sophisticated features. For example, although the first AID exemplar (Totterdell and Cooper, 1986) is adaptive - it stores a user history and has multiple responses to a given stimulus - it is not self- regulating. The exemplar offers a level of guidance to the user but it does this

Levels	Example Computer Systems
Adaptable/ tailorable	*Synics (Edmonds, 1981)*
Adaptive	*CONNECT(Alty, 1984a)* *Personalised directory (Greenberg & Witten, 1985)* *Adaptive indexing (Furnas, 1985)* *Adaptable manual (Mason & Thomas, 1984)* *PAL (Pickering et al., 1984)* *Dialog (Maskery, 1984)* *Poise (Croft, 1984)* *Monitor (Benyon, 1984)* *AID (Totterdell & Cooper, 1986)*
Self-regulating	*Document retrieval (Croft, 1984)* *LS - 1 (Smith, 1984)* *Telephone directory (Trevellyan & Browne, 1986)*
Self-mediating	------------
Self-modifying	------------

Fig 3.6 Taxonomy of computer adaptive systems

irrespective of whether or not they find the level of guidance useful, it does not evaluate the changes it makes to the interface.

The self regulating interface to the telephone directory referred to in Fig. 3.6 provides an example of the distinction between innate and learned adaptation. The interface has two strategies for structuring menus. The strategies and their conditions for use are already built into what Pylyshyn refers to as the functional architecture of the system. The adaptation is "independent of rule-governed construction from representations of relevant properties of the environment" (Pylyshyn, 1984) and represents an innate capacity, that is we cannot modify the beliefs of the system. In principle it would be possible to build an interface which varied its response and learnt, in the operant sense, when and when not to apply a strategy. However, the initial inefficiency of such a system would probably be unacceptable to its users and hence the decision to build the adaptive

Phase1 exemplar - An adaptive interface to electronic-mail

Phase 1 of the AID project produced an adaptive interface to an electronic mail system. The interface communicated with the mail system via a modem link. The interface's role was to select fragments of dialogue to suit the individual user. The fragments were selected according to a model of the user maintained in the interface. Cues in the user-system dialogue triggered changes in the model. The interface adapted along a number of dimensions.

-The guidance dimension adapted the prompting, feedback and level of help given to the user.

-The context dimension tracked users as they switched between tasks and set up their mail boxes to reflect previous interactions.

-The analagous mail dimension adapted the interface to accept commmands from an alternative command language

- And finally, the user tailoring dimension allowed users to define their own synonyms for commands and to adjust how fast the interface adapted along the guidance dimension.

---

capability into the functional architecture (as an innate capacity) rather than use a rule based representation of the environment.

DESIGN AS ADAPTATION

By examining the taxonomy more closely we can begin to draw some interesting conclusions about the design of adaptive systems. In fact we can see that the principal concern of design itself is adaptation; design is about constructing artifacts that are well-adapted to their environment.

Yates (1984) concluded from biological views of adaptation that adaptation is a hierarchical concept which must account in biology for both population and organismal adaptation. Population adaptation can, if looked at in the wider context, be viewed as the results of a larger adaptive system known as evolution which modifies and evaluates by the process of natural selection. The larger adaptive system is actually a design process. There is a parallel here with the current evolution of computer systems in which the most successful design features persist into the next generation. This is a general truth about all artifacts which pass through generations. There is also similarity between biological evolution and iterative design methodologies for human computer interfaces. In an iterative methodology, a prototype design is tested on potential end users and is then modified if necessary by an external agent, such as the interface designer, in order to improve the system's adaptedness.

We can see in the taxonomy that some of the design decisions normally made by the designer are being transferred to the self-adaptive system, and this is because it is not always possible to anticipate all contingencies that would make the system well adapted to its environment in advance of events. This leads to a further extension within the taxonomy, based on where the responsibility lies for taking design decisions. This applies to the range of design possibilities (variation), the one or more of these possibilities that have to be chosen (selection), and the design possibilities then have to be evaluated for their effectiveness (testing). The locus of responsibility for each facet lies with either the designer, the user or the system (Fig. 3.7) and this helps to determine how we classify a system within the taxonomy.

In a rapid-prototyping environment, the designer usually has responsibility for producing the variation (the design options), for selecting the best (the prototypes), and for testing them on users. In a tailorable system, the designer is still responsible for the variation but the design options are built into the system so that the user can select their preferred option; however, the actual success of the design options are still tested by the designer. The adaptive system and tailoring system have similar allocation of responsibility except that the adaptive system itself, and not the user, is responsible for selecting the design option. In a self regulating adaptive system the designer is responsible for the variation, the system is responsible for selecting the design and the system undertakes some of the testing (the overall success is tested by the designer). And finally, the self-modifying adaptive system takes responsibility for the variation as well as the selection and initial testing.

Level of system	Design facets		
	Variation	*Selection*	*Testing*
Designed	*Designer*	*Designer*	*Designer*
Adaptable/ tailorable	*Designer*	*User*	*Designer*
Adaptive	*Designer*	*System*	*Designer*
Self-regulating	*Designer*	*System*	*System*
Self-mediating	*Designer*	*System*	*System*
Self-modifying	*System*	*System*	*System*

Fig. 3.7 Principal design responsibilities within the taxonomy.

One trend in the taxonomy, therefore, is that as systems become more sophisticated they take on more of the responsibility for the three facets - first the variation, then the selection and finally the testing. However, shared responsibility is also possible and may define the style of the system; for example a system which has an underused capability to consult a user has an authoritarian style. The other trend which we can identify in the taxonomy is that as systems become more sophisticated they internalise much of the design work that used to occur between generations of systems.

USER INTERFACE DESIGN AS ADAPTATION

User interface design is a process of adapting the interface to the needs of its users, and where these are variable this process of adapting must be delegated to users or to an adaptive user interface (AUI) acting on the designer's behalf.

The term "deferred design" has been used in the AID project to refer to an approach where design decisions are deferred until the cues indicating which design variant is needed are available. Sometimes the appropriate user interface design cannot be decided at design time and the choice has to be deferred until run-time when the particular needs of a user become apparent, either because they are explicitly specified by the user (as in user tailoring) or because the interface infers the needs from implicit cues in the user's interactions.

The process of adapting to user needs starts with the initial product concept and continues through design, implementation, service and product upgrades. The particular concern of the AID project was adaptation of the user interface at run-time while the product is in service. Techniques developed in the project span the various levels - from user tailoring to automatic adaptation of the interface in response to changing users or changes in user needs. In principle, the same process of adapting the user interface is involved whether the designer, the user or the interface itself is the agent of change. It is up to the designer to decide between adapting the interface at design time, building in the means for the users to adapt the interface themselves at run-time or building in a mechanism able to choose the appropriate interface automatically at run-time. In the latter two cases, the designer delegates some of the design choices to the users or to an adaptive interface acting as a surrogate designer.

In practice designers have the following options:

(i)   they can search for a general design that is adapted to most users' needs or

(ii)   they can design the interface to incorporate the means for users to adapt the interface themselves or

(iii)   they can devise and build in mechanisms able to determine a user's particular needs and automatically adapt the interface accordingly or

(iv)   they can "adapt the users to the interface" by providing support for training users.

Adapting a user interface to its user's needs is a non-trivial task for the user interface designer. First they must recognise the variability in the needs of the users and show an adequate benefit in adapting to each variant. Then they must devise user interface designs adapted to each variant and have access to cues that indicate which variant of interface should be used in a given situation. And finally they must identify the agent of change. The options here are: designers who will practice multiple redesigns of the interface; or users who modify the interface through user tailoring; or self-adapting mechanisms which use internal run-time models (e.g. user and task models) to take decisions about changing the interface.

The "group adaptive interface" to "help" called Groupie is an example (Viliunas *et al.*, 1988) from the AID project which illustrates these points:

GROUPIE - an adaptive interface for HELP

Phase 2 and 3 of the AID project produced two different versions of an adaptive help facility called Groupie. Groupie was designed to allow a group of users to take the help provided on a system and tailor it to their own needs.
In particular, this allows experts (or gurus) who know the groups' help needs to add help "pitched" at the right level. Groupie then monitors the groups' use of the help messages and infers which ones are preferred. Preferred help messages are highlighted as a guide to other group members, particularly novices to the group. The groups' preferences may change over time and Groupie adapts to any changes by continually monitoring the use of help messages and changing its inferences accordingly.
Evaluation of Groupie (described in Chapter 6) showed that it was able to adapt its presentation of help messages to reflect the different requirements of different groups.
Groupie II differed from Groupie I in that the rating of the messages was assessed implicitly rather than explicitly on the basis of a "first past the post" voting scheme - see Chapter 5.

Different groups of users often vary in the help they need. But it is common for a group of users to include knowledgable experts, or gurus, who know the help needed. Ogborn and Johnson (1982) make the point that knowledge is something that is shared by a community, it is not the exclusive property of an individual and that the perpetuation and evolution of community knowledge is effected through the sharing and learning of this knowledge. However, tapping into the distributed knowledge or "folklore" of a group may not always be an easy way of obtaining appropriate help.

Consider options (i) to (iv) above:

(i)   It may be impossible for the designer to provide help appropriate for every group of users.

(ii)   By providing gurus with the means to add help tailored to the group, the provision of appropriate help can be delegated to expert users. The interface also allows each user to choose their own preferred help, e.g. that of their preferred guru.

(iii)   Furthermore, by monitoring users' choice of help, the system can detect which help seems most useful to users. These cues are then used to automatically adapt the default choice of help to either that preferred by an individual user or to that preferred by the group (i.e. most users in the group).

(iv)   Such a scheme provides support for training users to individual or group needs.

The final choice of design will depend on the relative costs and benefits of the alternatives, and how practical and acceptable (to its users) each alternative proves to be. The Groupie interface has focused on options (ii) and (iii). Some of the benefits of these options may be that:

-   They relieve the designer from the burden of understanding local help requirements.

-   They encourage the development of group norms (Maude *et al.*, 1984) and the natural use of simplifying assumptions and cliches (Rich and Waters, 1982).

-   They provide a centralised source of tailored help for the community and promote a sense of community spirit.

ADAPTIVE INTERFACE ARCHITECTURE

Taking the four design options in the previous section, it can be seen that:

In (i) the designer is the agent of change and so builds models of the user population using cues gleaned from users. This leads to an understanding, or theory, of their needs. Since for (i) a single fixed user interface design is assumed to meet the needs of all its users, the designer can eventually settle on and implement one all-embracing variant of the design (although many designs may be considered and adapted by the designer during the design process).

In (ii) the users are the agent of change, and select from the interface variants provided by the designer to suit their (possibly changing) needs. This means that users must understand for themselves which interface variant is best suited to their particular needs. In effect they have to "understand" the theory and how to put it into practice at the user interface. To do this a user has to model, in his or her head, the current situation as it changes.

In (iii) the user interface is the agent of change. Therefore, as well as providing the interface variants, the designer needs to automate: the detection of cues to a user's needs, the modelling of those needs as they relate to the theory, and the choice of user interface variant according to the theory. This is by far the most difficult option for the designer because it involves building a mechanism capable of inferring when and how to change the interface on the evidence of implicit cues in the user's interactions with the interface. But for the user, if it can be made to work, this option relieves him or her of the burdens described above.

In contrast, option (iv) places the entire burden of adapting on the user; with the designer, at best, providing cues in the form of automated help or training.

The process of adapting a user interface to current user needs requires the following, regardless of who or what acts as the agent of change:

- A theory underlying the adaptation which relates user behaviour to user interface needs.

- Access to behavioural cues in user interactions from which a need for one rather than another interface design variant can be inferred according to the theory.

- The flexibility in the user interface to accommodate each design variant.

- Models which accumulate the evidence of cues and represent a particular need to the agent of change.

- An agent of change to make the appropriate design choice on the evidence according to the theory.

This is shown diagrammatically in Fig. 3.8, where the agent of

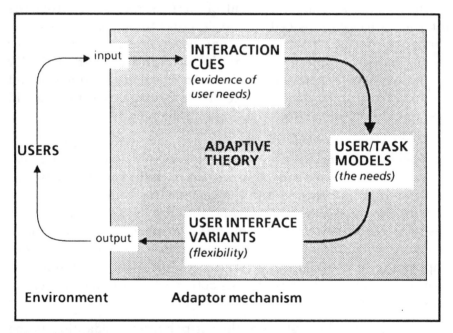

Fig. 3.8 Logical architecture of adaptation in a User Interface.

change is represented by the bold arrows.

Some of the adaptive interfaces developed in the AID project used more than one level of architecture for adaptation - corresponding to the higher levels in the taxonomy of adaptive systems . A lower level adaptor, driven by short-term cues, adapts the interface to track short-term changes in circumstances (i.e. user need) according to a "current" theory. A second, higher-level adaptor controls the first by monitoring longer-term characteristics of user needs and adapts, not the user interface itself, but the current theory controlling the lower-level adaptor. This two-level arrangement corresponds to a two-level theory: a higher level theory which identifies the most appropriate variant of a lower level theory for adapting the user interface to the prevailing user needs. By splitting the theory into two levels, the lower level can concentrate on the transient characteristics of user needs while the higher level concentrates on identifying major changes in user needs which would be beyond the scope of any single lower level theory. The resulting architecture shown in Fig. 3.9 is, not surprisingly, similar to that found in adaptive control systems (e.g. Arbib, 1972).

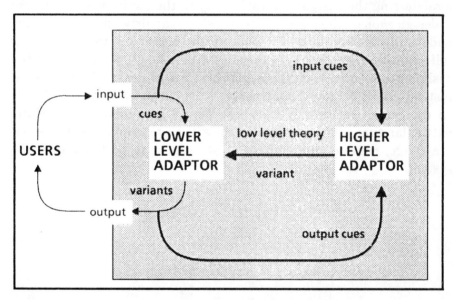

Fig. 3.9 Two level architecture for adaptation.

The higher level adaptor evaluates the performance of the alternative lower level theories by monitoring the input/output behaviour (interaction cues) at the user interface. The performance is assessed against the objective of adaptation using specific metrics of user performance. The best lower level theory for a given situation is then chosen on the basis of the performance metrics.

CONCLUSION

In the AID project we have used the term "deferred design" to describe the approach of leaving design decisions open, by building the design variants into the system, until the cues are available to indicate which design variant is needed. Adaptive interfaces are the means by which we can achieve deferred design.

The role of adaptive systems is to gain power of functioning by reacting to environmental variety. To achieve this they must be sensitive to different requirements. These requirements cannot always be anticipated and hence the need for flexible mechanisms. The design of these mechanisms must give an account of: the *reasons* for deferring the design (the variability in the environment), the set of design *choices*, the *triggers* or cues which can drive the mechanism, and finally the *metrics* for evaluating the benefits of the design. As self adaptive systems are developed it will no longer be the task of the designer to identify the design that best fits a "generic" set of users; instead it will be the responsibility of the run-time system to decide on the design or strategy that best fits the individual user at any particular time. The designer's role will be to take decisions about the range, content and control of strategies to be built into the system.

Chapter 4
Methods for Building Adaptive Systems

D. Browne, M. Norman and E. Adhami

Previous chapters have introduced an approach which raises relevant questions regarding the desired behaviour of an adaptive system and discussed a taxonomy and architecture for adaptive interfaces. To satisfy the requirements of constructing adaptive interfaces several key methods have been identified which can support their design and implementation. An adaptive system needs a means of modelling the variability on which the adaptation will be based; such means are usually termed USER MODELS, and the use of these is reviewed. Additionally, to permit change of the user interface, it is essential that flexibility is built into the user interface software through some DIALOGUE MODEL. Suitable dialogue specification methods are reviewed. Variability is often very context dependent, usually being dependent on the particular task being undertaken. This creates a need for a TASK MODEL. A task modelling tool is described. It is widely appreciated that separation of user interface concerns from purely functional concerns is good software engineering practice (Green, 1984). To maintain such a separation requires an APPLICATION MODEL, and the project's use of such a model is reviewed.

USER MODELLING

To quote from Gaines (1972), "A controller does not generally change its state instantaneously according to the state of the environment, and the manner in which it changes state is a function not only of the immediate environment but also of its previous states. It is this sequential dependence, or memory, inherent in the behaviour of most adaptive systems, which gives rise to transfer effects in training, and indeed, to most of the complexity of adaptive behaviour." As this quote states, adaptive systems temper their changes across changing environments, hence the need for a model of variability in the environment.

The necessity for a user model in any adaptive system or at least those subset of adaptive systems that react to user variability, is a consequence of the need to maintain a history of the user's interaction with the system. It is this history which provides a profile of the user which can then be used to reason about the most suitable individualised interface. This profile is not necessarily the same as the stereotyping approach proposed by Rich (1979), but usually a more linear depiction of some aspect or aspects of the user population's variability.

At present it would be impossible to build user models that maintained a view on all types of variability (although Kass & Finin (1988) have developed a General User Modelling System (GUMS) facility for supporting cooperative advisory systems). That is why in Chapter 2, pains were taken to discriminate types of variability and encourage the builders of adaptive systems to recognise their particular frames of reference.

It should be stated that every system encapsulates an implicit user model. In specifying any system, the designer possesses a view, however poor or inaccurate, of the intended users of that system. Rarely is this view concretised in a model. Moran (1981) argues that this is exactly what should be required of designers and proposes a set of abstractions and a notation to encourage the rigorous documentation of the user model from a task-oriented or behavioural standpoint. User modelling as discussed below, concentrates on models for the sole objective of recording user variability in a manner that can be reasoned about in order to provide a dynamic user interface.

User models can be categorised in a number of ways. Browne (1987), Daniels (1986), and Carroll and McKendree (1987) are just three examples. The following discussion will use the Browne (1987) categorisation with references to counterparts in the other categorisations and examples of existing systems that have embedded user models.

Static Updatable Models

Some models are static in that the model itself does not change. A single model is used and applied to every user. The only way in which user differences are captured is in terms of which parts of the model are "set". For instance, a concept attainment model might simply be updated in terms of the concepts that users are familiar with. Thus for one user the model might indicate that their knowledge of a particular part of the system was very scant while another user had a very good understanding of the operating system but a poor knowledge of the editor. These differences would then be used to provide an appropriately individualised user interface. With this type of modelling a single model is employed for all users although its affects will be different for each individual depending on their previous interaction with the system.

An example is the UMFE (User Modelling Front-End) system (Sleeman, 1985). UMFE provides tailored explanation about the NEOMYCIN system; which is an expert system for medical diagnosis. The user model begins as a semantic net of concepts and the dialogue includes questions to determine the concepts a user will understand. The model is updated by deletion of concepts that UMFE infers the user will not comprehend. The updated model then provides a basis for tailoring explanations to the individual.

The distinction between static updatable models and other types of model is that they begin by partitioning the task space. Pure "static updatable models" would take no account of enduring user differences, only the quantity and possibly quality of an individual's interaction with a systems dialogue component. From these interactions, users are pigeonholed with respect to those components. By such means a user could be conceived as a novice at editing but an expert at file management. This certainly has an intuitive appeal. No one is "Jack of all trades". But there must also be misgivings about such a pure approach given that transfer of knowledge from one task to another is likely to affect the quality of interaction (Polson *et al.*, 1987); these misgivings being particularly valid in large application areas encompassing highly related tasks.

Comparison Models

A more common approach is the utilisation of two models. One is static and not updatable. This is similar to normative models in Carroll & McKendree's (1987) breakdown and represents expert or expected usage of the system. The second model may be a static updatable model or a dynamic model that characterises some dimension or dimensions of user variability. The result of comparing the two models provides a basis for user interface changes.

Examples of systems that use comparison of models predominate in the Computer Aided Learning area. For instance, Sleeman (1982) used an idealised expert model as a comparator for an algebra tutor. The approach was found successful: it made relevant diagnoses on 50% of occasions and provided a correct prognosis for 50% of these.

WURSOR III (Goldstein, 1982) compares a model of actual system usage against a model of expertise in playing the game of WUMPUS. Players of the game have to find and kill the dangerous animal known as the WUMPUS. Depending on the fit between the two models, the user is attributed with a skill level. This in turn is used within WURSOR III to choose suitable explanations, subsequent topics and determine how well a student knows a rule.

As pointed out by Daniels (1986): "Many systems have too wide a field of application to be able to form a representation of an 'ideal' user ..." In addition, as suggested earlier, classifying users on the basis of interactions with a subset of a system and then generalising the use of this classification could be invalid.

Alternative Models

Rather than comparing models in order to classify users, a number of rules can be used to choose a model that best characterises a user. These models are themselves static, mirroring enduring characteristics of the users that they are describing. Unlike comparison models that anticipate changes within the individual, alternative models assume longevity of individual characteristics. For instance, the simplest case would be to have a rule of the form:

IF a user displays characteristics A and B, THEN use model X ELSE use model Y.

Of course, by testing the rules more frequently during interaction, the behaviour of the model will be similar to that of a comparison model. The choice really depends on the anticipated duration of the characteristic and the confidence with which one model can be chosen over another.

Fowler *et al.* (1985) provide evidence for the applicability of employing alternative models. Their study examined the relationship between the cognitive style dimension of field independence (Witkin & Goodenough, 1981) and dialogue style. Their results showed that field dependent persons prefer a substructured command language while field independent persons prefer a linear command language. Given that field independence is an enduring individual characteristic, it would seem plausible to have alternative models for these two classes of users. Of course, in this particular case - or indeed with all cognitive and personality dimensions - the major difficulty is how to categorise people unobtrusively.

Plan-Recognition-Based Modelling

These models describe the tasks or plans (Sridharan, 1985) that a user might be expected to attempt; they take no account of individual differences. At a top level, the model may consider a user's goal to be one of learning a query system or a new command language. Intermediate goals are derived by using a model of the tasks the user wishes to accomplish. The identification of such intermediate goals would then allow the provision of a user interface that encourages the accomplishment of the user's immediate goal. For example, an error in using a single command would produce different feedback depending on the user's present goal. This type of modelling was employed with mixed success in the AID project's first attempt to build an adaptive user interface (Totterdell & Cooper 1986). One means of establishing whether such an approach is likely to reap dividends is to analyse recordings of user interactions in the application domain of interest. While the recording is running the designer should attempt to second guess what the user will attempt subsequently, that is identify their goals. If they have little success, then it is unlikely that they will be able to produce a plan recognition based user model that will be successful.

Usage Models

Possibly one of the simplest means of modelling for the provision of an adaptive user interface is to employ usage models. Such models pay little or no attention to user differences at any level other than the usage made of information within the system. That is, they pay no attention to intrinsic user differences. The information obtainable from the system is not modelled either. Each information item is treated similarly, only its quantifiable utilisation being of importance. One of the best examples of this type of modelling is given by Greenberg & Witten (1985). On the basis of a user's information access patterns - specifically to items in an on-line telephone directory - the content of menus in a hierarchy of menus was altered. These alterations afforded a decrease in the average number of key presses required to retrieve frequently accessed items of information.

A replication and extension to this study by Trevellyan and Browne (1987) replicated the findings and demonstrated that adaptive success - actual number of keypresses - could be monitored and used as another source of data for adaptation. This study will be elaborated in Chapter 6.

As suggested, the above five categories of user model can be considered independently. The choice of the most appropriate one will need to be taken on a case by case basis. "Existing literature on systems that incorporate an explicit user model show that the majority of the sytems are closely tied to their domain of application" (Clowes et al., 1985). The most suitable modelling technique will depend on what user variability or inferred individual differences are to be modelled, and on the purpose of the adaptation. To complicate the issue further, the need for different types of adaptation within a single application may give rise to different modelling needs. For instance, it may be desirable to use a comparison model during the early phases of application usage followed by, or in tandem with, a choice of alternate models that categorise users on some cognitive function dimension. This would enable adaptation to both transient and enduring characteristics of the user.

Alternative breakdowns of user models do exist, as stated previously. One particularly useful dimension suggested by Daniels (1985) is the separation between dynamic and static models. To quote Daniels: dynamic models are "context-dependent changing models from the system's point of view, and refer to changes of user state which are dependent on interaction with the system. Static models represent permanent features of users which are independent of the behaviour of the system, and are consistent over the session". This distinction is similar to that made earlier between models that describe enduring user characteristics as opposed to transitory or developing characteristics. The noteworthy point in Daniel's quote is the context dependency of dynamic models. At present, research on the importance of context and how knowledge of context might usefully be employed is only sparsely researched (Douglas, 1987).

At present, context as modelled by systems is usually implicit. For purposes of adaptation, task modelling appears to be as strong a contextual factor as technology will permit cognizance of. The very richness of contextual information that users bring to bear on interaction and the historical immensity on which these interactions are based will be beyond computational limitations for some time to come. This is why user modelling at present is limited to inferring properties from very incomplete data.

USER INTERFACE MODELLING

Having discussed user modelling, it now seems appropriate to discuss how to support the user interface that this modelling is going to affect. For reasons of expediency, discussion will be confined to tools available; usually known as User Interface Management Systems (UIMS). Each of these employs a user interface model, the best known of which is the Seeheim model (Green, 1986), shown in Fig. 4.1. The user interface model is the basis for the specification notations. According to Green (1986):

"The range of a design notation can be measured in two ways. The descriptive power of a notation is the set of user interfaces that can

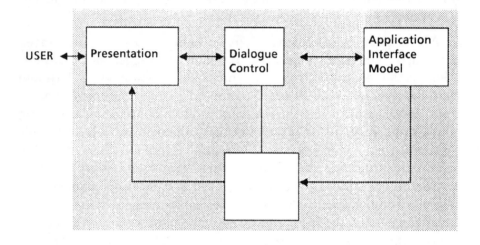

Fig. 4.1 Seeheim model.

be described by the notation.The second way...... is by its usable
power."

Essentially notations can be assessed by the range of user interfaces
that can be specified by them and by the difficulty of the specification
process. Guest (1982) showed that students of varying computer
literacy were less likely to accept a notation that they perceived to be
complex. Obviously ease of use will affect the acceptance of any
notation, but its descriptive power is likely to be a more pervasive
determinant of its value in the design of an adaptive user interface.
Designing adaptive user interfaces is inherently difficult, the extra
overhead of learning a notation is unlikely to be dissuading if the
efficacy of the notation with regard to adaptation is apparent.

To date the Dialogue Control component of User Interface models
has received most concerted attention. Three dialogue models with
supporting notations will be discussed. These being: state transition
networks, context-free grammars and event based notations. Each of
these will be described in turn with examples of UIMS that utilise
them. Where possible the value of each with respect to adaptive user
interface design and implementation will be discussed.

State Transition Networks.

A state transition network is composed of nodes and directed arcs. Nodes are usually depicted as circles and these represent the "state" of dialogue between user and computer. In their simplest form arcs are labelled with input tokens. The dialogue will progress from state to state as input tokens are received that appear on arcs linking the present state to a possible future state. As can be seen in Fig. 4.2, if

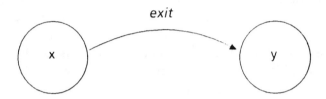

Fig. 4.2 State transition network.

the dialogue has reached state x and the user provides the token "exit" then the dialogue will assume state y. In this way user tasks can be described as a sequence of arcs linking some starting state to some final state possibly by traversal of some intermediate states. Computer actions can be linked to either nodes or arcs, or even both. Green (1984) points to two problems of transition diagrams: firstly, only a limited range of dialogues can be described by them and the descriptions tend to get rather large. This latter problem is often ameliorated by using subdiagrams. A subdiagram is a complete transition network in its own right that can be invoked from another diagram. Subdiagrams may even be allowed to call themselves giving them a recursive property.

Augmented recursive transition networks also include registers and functions. The registers can hold data values that act like local variables. Functions can read and write to these registers. By attaching functions to arcs they can be used to control the traversal of the network. The use of registers and functions can render networks context sensitive. A simple example might be the existence of a register that holds a value representing how often a point in the network has been traversed. An associated function might then control the direction of the dialogue based on this value. For instance, it could direct the dialogue down a path that provides in-depth explanation factilities if the network has been infrequently traversed.

The major attraction of state transition networks is their graphical representation. Dialogue designers seem more at ease using graphics in order to specify interaction than they do using grammars or highly symbolic character-based notations. Wasserman & Shewmake (1984) specifically chose to implement their User Software Engineering (USE) method as transition networks rather than Backus-Naur Form (BNF). Among the reasons for that decision were the readability of such diagrams compared with BNF, thereby easing communication with users. USE has a number of interesting extensions. The concept of subdiagrams is implemented in USE as subconversations. USE generated diagrams are implementable; that is they have associated semantics. Variables can be included in the diagrams and these can be type checked. Actions can be associated with arcs with branching dependent on the outcome of the action. Output to the user is facilitated by format control constructs for such things as inverse video, scrolling and cursor positioning. In addition user input can be handled in various ways such as by truncation, identification of special characters, and recognition of time outs.

Kamran & Feldman (1983) proposed an interaction language based on augmented state transition networks and implemented as a finite state machine equivalent. In a self-critique of this work Kamran (1985) made a point of obvious relevance given our interest in adaptive systems, namely that:

> "The sequencing of user-level tasks .. should, in general, be flexible and adaptable to the needs of individual users. The User Interface Designer ... should be able to 'program' this flexible sequencing and any restrictions on it, using the Interaction Language."

This same point was clearly in the minds of the developers of CONNECT (Alty, 1984a, b) CONNECT uses both state transition networks and production rules. According to Alty networks are "easily understood by designers" although "they tend to be large and inflexible." In addition, he states, "Production Rules are more versatile but are difficult to check for correctness and cannot be subjected easily to theoretical analysis." The power of the CONNECT system was derived from coalescing these two approaches. The dialogue was represented as transition networks that can be analysed using path algebras (Carre, 1971; Backhouse & Carre, 1975) to derive properties such as loops, step-lengths and appropriate subnets. The production rules permit the topology of the network to be changed during interaction on the basis of data gleaned from monitoring interaction. In this way the dialogue can be adapted by "opening or closing" existing arcs, thus forcing interaction down certain paths.

The major attraction of transition networks appears to be their visual clarity. Dialogue structure and sequence can easily be assimilated. Transition network editors facilitate the easy modification and maintenance of such networks. Unfortunately most UIMS based on transition networks are limited in their descriptive power; they are inadequate for describing concurrent dialogues and often poor in their ability to describe context.

Context-free Grammars.

A prime example of a context-free grammar is Backus Naur Form (BNF) (Naur, 1963). Such grammars consist of at least the following:

- a set of terminal symbols, which are the words of the language,

- a set of non-terminal symbols to represent the structure of the language,

- a starting symbol,

- meta-symbols for operations such as "and", "or", and "is composed of", and

- rules constructed from the above.

Reisner (1981) and Schneiderman (1982) used extended BNF notations to describe user interfaces. Reisner's "action grammars" were used to describe the input languages to the ROBART 1 and ROBART 2 interactive colour graphics systems. The resulting notations were then used to predict the performance of users interacting with each of the systems. User errors were successfully predicted on the basis of identifying complex or inconsistent BNF rules. This implies the possibility of identifying design shortcomings during specification of an interface. Schneiderman altered the BNF slightly so that non-terminal symbols could be associated with user or computer (multi-party grammars) and with one anomaly could also be mapped directly onto state transition networks.

Payne & Green (1983), recognised that BNF-style notations cannot represent the similarity between rules. They therefore proposed a set grammar to identify inconsistencies in an interface specification.

There are a number of other difficulties posed by such grammars. Firstly, they are cumbersome in that a complete notation for an average-sized interface will be rather lengthy and probably have little obvious structure. Secondly, partly because of the absence of structure it can be difficult to ascertain when something will occur, that is, which input tokens need to be recognised. Thirdly, as a consequence of the above, it becomes difficult to specify prompts, help messages and error messages. In addition, it is difficult to specify concurrent dialogues and context within such grammars.

Olsen and Dempsey (1983) used an extended BNF in SYNGRAPH, a graphical user interface generator. The extensions to BNF allowed for optional phrases, repeating phrases, and alternation. These were added to "allow non-terminals to be used to organize the dialogue rather than as a recursive control structure." SYNGRAPH specifically provides facilities for specifying user prompting, provision of help, error detection, undo and returning to a known state.

More recently, Scott & Yap (1988) proposed an extended context-free grammar for dialogues which addresses the issue of concurrency and context. Concurrency is handled using a fork operator. This operator can be used to activate sub-parsers that operate in parallel. Context is handled by insisting that all tokens have at least two attributes: value and context. Value describes a token's type while context denotes the source of a token, for instance a particular screen window. The notation is based on LL(1) grammars which purportedly are "easy to read for humans, without any puzzles or surprises....", (Grune and Jacobs, 1988).

Event Model of User Interaction.

The origins of event-based user interface management systems are in graphics work, particularly the work on device drivers. For instance, mouse movements are treated as named events with associated parameters for the coordinates of the cursor. UIMS based on the event model recognise events generated by the user, the application, or from internal components such as the dialogue controller. Each event is sent to a process known as an event handler, a number of which may exist. Such handlers can perform some computation, kill and generate event handlers, and call application procedures. The behaviour of an event handler is defined using a template or form that includes its input parameters, local variables, scope and response to events. Any form can be used to generate a number of event handlers, each with a unique name and possibly unique parameters and variable values.

At run-time an initial form is automatically generated. It serves as the main event handler, generating other event handlers which may in turn generate others. Event handlers can be thought of as executing concurrently although any one handler can only deal with one event at a time. They can also be considered as monitors for events because each one can declare in advance those events it will process.

ALGAE (Flecchia & Bergeron, 1987) was developed to 'fit' the Seeheim user interface model as shown in Fig. 4.3. Event handlers reside in each of the three main components; all communication is via event passing. In effect this means that each component could be handled by a separate process, possibly residing on different machines. Events are structures having a type and a value. Events of different structure can be handled by a single event handler. Handlers wait for events to occur, service them and then wait for another event.

ALGAE supports two comparatively complex and often desirable user interface facilities. Firstly, it permits dialogue to be stacked. That is a dialogue can be suspended and later re-established. An obvious requirement for this is in interrupting an application to respond to user initiated requests for help. Secondly, multithreaded dialogues can be supported. Such dialogues have the properties of

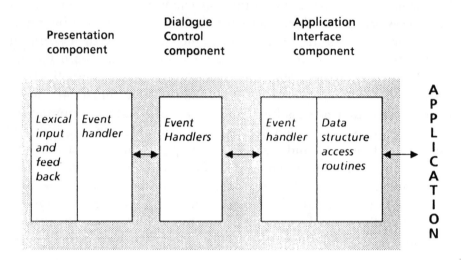

Fig. 4.3 ALGAE user interface model.

running concurrently and possibly interacting with each other. Multi-threaded dialogues are most prevalent in window-based systems, where interaction in one window may affect another window.

Hill (1986), proposed an Event-Response Language (ERL) as an improvement over augmented transition networks. ERL renders specifications of concurrent dialogues compact and maintainable. In addition, such specifications can be interpreted or compiled effectively. Resulting ERL processors take incoming events and produce events in the same manner as event handlers in ALGAE. Each ERL processor may have a set of flags or local variables that hold "state" information and also control execution.

Sassafras (Hill, 1987) utilises the facilities of the Interlisp-D programming environment to provide a user interface prototyping system on top of the ERL specification language. It provides an icon library and icon builder. Interaction techniques, or mini dialogues are implemented as interaction modules. Sassafras provides the means for producing a specification of the application interface, and an interface assembler to link the dialogue specification with the other components. In addition, Sassafras takes the approach of sharing control between the user interface and the application rather than one or other having complete control.

One of the main benefits of the event based modelling approach is the relative ease with which concurrent dialogues can be specified and implemented. For cooperative interfaces, adaptive interfaces or what might be termed "agency" style interfaces, concurrent dialogues are a real requirement. In addition, the consideration of event handlers as "monitors", possibly for triggers to adaptation modules is very much in keeping with the requirements of any architecture for an adaptive system.

However, the advantages of the event based modelling approach are tempered by Scott and Yaps' (1988) comments:

"Event handlers have the drawback that the input/output language cannot readily be determined without inspecting handler code. Clarity also suffers from the fact that an event may activate more than one handler. It may not be easy to determine which handlers will be active at any given time. Finally, because they so closely resemble program code themselves, event handlers provide relatively little opportunity for labor-saving compilation. The abstraction level of grammars is significantly higher."

Three of the main dialogue modelling techniques have been described. No attempt is made to prescribe that one modelling technique is better than another with regard to building adaptive systems. It should be apparent that the choice of one rather than another should be made on a case by case appraisal. The type of dialogue modelling technique required really depends on the type of user interface to be supported, particularly with respect to the type of adaptation to be provided. For example, for adaptation at an intertask level a state transition network may be appropriate. But for adaptation at a finer level of granularity an event based model would be more suitable. Both have been found useful on the AID project.

Just to complicate the issue further a new generation of UIMS is evolving (Myers & Buxton, 1986, Olsen, 1986, Olsen & Dance, 1988). While these UIMS still acknowledge and in many respects adhere to the logic of the Seeheim model they completely reverse the user interface development cycle. Rather than following a specify, refine and implement sequence, the functionality of the interface is defined first, then the visual appearance is prototyped and finally its syntax is derived. Thus, in systems like the Menu Interaction Kontrol Environment (MIKE, Olsen, 1986) the interface is defined by means of an interface editor rather than a textual specification. Interestingly, the approach enables a separation of concerns during design:

> "If the design group can first decide on the semantics of what the user interface should do, the application programmers can then begin designing how these commands are to be implemented. Meanwhile, the human-factors experts can work on how the commands are visually and interactively expressed."

The advantages that can be gained from a separation of concerns is reinforced later in this chapter by the experiences of the AID project in relation to application modelling.

TASK MODELLING

As stated previously, one of the major difficulties in providing adaptive user interfaces is quite simply the diversity of sources of information that can affect the appropriate choice of a design variant. We have concentrated our discussions on the variability of the end-user. In most circumstances modelling these characteristics is unlikely to be sufficient. For instance, the state of the system itself and states of the world external to the system are likely to affect a user's behaviour *per se*, or what would be deemed appropriate behaviour if only they were cognizant of this state information. Quite simply, a user's behaviour, or desired behaviour, is extremely context sensitive. Given that the building of adaptive user interfaces aims to improve the quality of human performance, it is desirable to consider the context of performance. This can be aided by undertaking a task analysis.

Task analysis provides a description of the activities undertaken by human operators when performing their jobs. This description is usually based on documentary evidence, interviews, observation and protocol analysis. The deliverable is a behavioural description of tasks, and can take a number of forms. However there are relatively few tried and tested task analysis methods.

Task analysis is commonly used as the basis for modelling human performance. In the case of adaptive systems the need for such modelling is most apparent in the building of user models. We shall see later that it can also play a role in application modelling. Task analysis for adaptive systems requires: a method for conducting the analysis, a notation for documenting the results of the analysis, and a mechanism for imbuing the adaptive system with an "awareness" of tasks. We shall look at each of these requirements in turn.

Conducting a Task Analysis

Johnson *et al.* (1988) propose each of the following as having a potential role in a task analysis:

- analysis of texts or manuals   - frequency counting
- direct observation of task performer - rating scales;
- analyst performing task   - sorting
- structured interview with task performer - list ordering
- questionnaire   - pilot study
- direct observation of task performer - tutorial sessions
- concurrent or retrospective protocol

To this list could also be added:

- prototype walk-throughs
- process model walk-throughs
- repertory grid analysis
- soft systems methodology

The objective of any analysis method is to describe the activities of the task performer and where possible the relevant dimensions of the environment in which the analysis was conducted. This produces a characterisation of the performer's procedures, related objects and their attributes, actions and plans. The sources for such information are obviously the task performers and others (manuals, data sources, folklore, etc.) that impact the tasks undertaken. Task analysis methods are intended to permit the characterisation of tasks and their interdependencies such that, given the state of the system, a prediction can be made regarding the likely subsequent states and actions of the performer. The state of the system includes both human and machine and quite possibly external factors. The state of the human at any time may include intentions, beliefs and goals to be achieved. The state of the machine may include the point reached in a dialogue, the information it has available and possible future states. Some of these factors can be quite nebulous and this is why any task analyst must use a variety of methods to unearth the relevant factors and their interconnections and implications.

Interviewing is the most frequently used method. Usually conducted in a structured fashion, that is with a number of specific questions to be answered, interviewing can provide a good overview of tasks in a relatively short period of time. In order for interviews to be structured it is often necessary to prepare by reviewing any texts or manuals associated with the job being analysed. Such reviews can also help to provide the analyst with an appropriate vocabulary so that the interview is not undermined by frequent diversions into discourse about terminology. Impartiality is however a problem in interviewing.

Direct observation of tasks has the advantage of apparent objectivity. The analyst simply records what is seen. A number of problems still exist though. Firstly, the analyst can only record an interpretation of events. There is no guarantee that important influences on the task are not being missed. A further problem, or phenomenon is the Hawthorne effect (Rotheliesberg & Dickson, 1939). The fact that an analyst is observing, no matter how unobtrusively, affects what is seen. The latter of these problems cannot be circumvented, but the first can be somewhat ameliorated. If a recording, either handwritten or preferably videotaped, of the situation can be made then the analyst can later discuss and review the recording with the performer. A further alternative, although similar, is to ask the performer to provide a concurrent explanation of what they are doing and why. Berry and Broadbent (1984), found that concurrent vocalisation affected task performance.

Another set of techniques may be used to gain further insights into tasks. Frequency counting, list ordering and rating scales are used to characterise the relative importance of tasks or more particularly task related objects and their attributes. Some of these techniques may seem removed from the activities of interest, and thus of limited value, but they can provide insights and can be used for validating the results of other task analysis techniques. Kelly's repertory grid method, originally developed for personality testing (Kelly, 1955), has now been adapted for use by knowledge engineers (Shaw, 1982; Shaw & Gaines, 1987). Its aim is to uncover the "mental" constructs that people use when considering a particular domain.

Pilot studies and prototyping can also be used in the later stages of task analysis, more as confirmation or validation aids than as initial analysis techniques. Pilot studies make use of specially chosen "props". For instance, in order to understand the task of finding faults in a drainage system the analyst might use plans of drains plus a set of symptoms. These would then provide a framework for asking drainage engineers about their problem solving behaviour. In this way the analyst can validate many possible scenarios without having to await their natural occurence. Similarly, prototypes can be used to analyse possible situations.

Process model walk-throughs are another means of validating an analysis. Where the analyst has a reasonably clear depiction of the job being performed it can be documented, usually graphically, as a set of procedures to be followed. Decision points in the process model can then be used as junctures at which the performer can be questioned further while stepping through the process model. In this way the model can be checked for correctness and completeness.

Smolensky et al. (1984) used the method of constructive interaction (O'Malley et al., 1984 Miyake, 1982) in an attempt to "formalise", printing tasks. This method requires observation of more than one individual cooperating to accomplish a task, or set of tasks. The rationale is that cooperating individuals will provide a more natural verbal protocol than a lone individual. The individuals should be of comparable knowedge with regard to the topic, they should be motivated to "solving" the problem, and the emphasis should be on comprehension not simply procedural accomplishment. Smolensky *et al.* found the method useful in confirming their "formal" descriptions. The technique was supplemented by analysis of actual on-line usage of the commands pertinent to the activities under consideration.

One further method is Checkland's (1981) Soft Systems Methodology (SSM). One of the premises of this approach is that two people may have different constructs for the task domain and even people with similar constructs may organise them differently. SSM, unlike some other methods, explicitly acknowledges individual variability. The "soft" aspect comes from the acknowledgement that there is no single "right"'answer for a given situation. Checkland's work reinforces the earlier point that analysts should not bring preconceived ideas to an analysis. Our use of soft systems analysis was restricted to interviewing and preparing rich pictures of many performers of "document preparation" tasks. Immediately following each interview idealised pictures, see for example Fig. 4.4, were drawn to depict the tasks performed, the important objects and attributes of the tasks, and relationships between them. The pictures keep the analyst free from any notations that might detract from the recording of the interviews or straight-jacket the findings. Because of the freedom of expression encouraged by this method it is easier to capture the differences between individuals regarding how they perform their tasks.

All of the above methods have a potential role in task analysis. The choice depends on many factors, including access to the job performer, the complexity of the job, and the objectives of the analysis. For adaptive systems the method should allow the analyst to document the alternative means by which tasks can be performed, including the different means individuals would use and if possible the determinants of one rather than another. For our work on adaptive systems for document preparation, Checkland's soft systems methodology seemed particularly useful for identifying task alternatives. These alternatives then enabled us to identify opportunities for adaptive user interfaces. The next stage is to document the results of the task analysis method unambiguously.

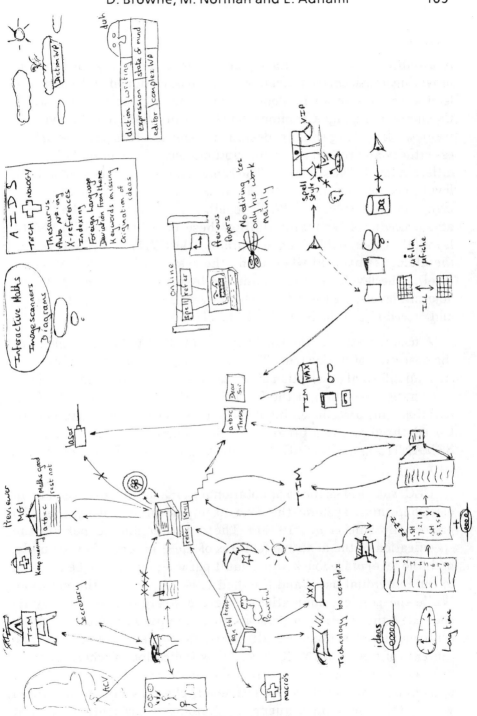

Fig 4.4 Rich pictures

Task Analysis Notations.

A number of notations have been proposed for the purpose of providing a task characterisation that can be critiqued and which will lead effectively to an implementation. Among the best known is Command Language Grammar (CLG, Moran, 1981). CLG provides a framework for organising design decisions. This framework is essentially an ordered set of descriptions, each description being at a different level of abstraction. The same basic notation is used at each level. The four levels used by Moran cover: the tasks which the user brings to the system (the TASK level), the objects within the system and procedures for manipulating these objects (the SEMANTIC level), the command language available (the SYNTACTIC level), and the dialogue involved when using the system (the INTERACTION level). The levels are then connected by means of mappings across adjacent levels, e.g the TASK level descriptions are linked to objects and procedures at the SEMANTIC level (Moran, 1983).

A useful feature of the CLG approach is that the levels "open up" the operation of the system. The structure provides a way of moving from an informal description of the task through various mappings to a concrete description at the INTERACTION level. Using the CLG notation, the procedures involved with specific user tasks can be traced through their progressive development as METHODS at SEMANTIC and SYNTACTIC levels to the actual dialogue with the user.

CLG was used as the task notation for an adaptive front-end to an electronic mail system; the first exemplar produced by the AID project (Browne *et al.*, 1986). The notation had to permit the specification of the adaptive features of the front-end. For example, both the level of feedback and default parameters were to be adapted to the individual users and this had to be reflected in the notation. While the possible adaptations here are straightforward, they do show how the location of presentations, the use of defaults and the confirmation of actions are all linked to the levels in CLG. The contents of the SEMANTIC level allow indication of where to place presentations and feedback in relation to the sequence of task operations. At the SYNTACTIC level, changes are incorporated within the command sequences. Automatic presentations that replace possible commands from the user, confirmative feedback that adds information onto a command at a particular location in a task, and the possible selection of defaults are all represented at this level. The INTERACTION level then shows how these changes are integrated into the dialogue between user and system. An obvious feature of the levels is that the change points can be situated at consistent locations within the sequence of user actions, and "units" for adaptation can be identified. For our purposes, the "units" were user tasks, with the changes being enabled at task boundaries.

CLG suffers from a number of deficiencies. For example, it does not yet have a presentation layer permitting easy specification of screen layouts and it does not have suitable primitives for interfaces other than ones in a command based style. For adaptive interfaces in particular a number of specific limitations were identified.

At the SYNTACTIC level the idea of a state variable that is "active inside the command context in which it is defined" (Moran, 1981, p.16) is introduced. To aid the building of adaptive interfaces it would be beneficial to have a similar concept to state variable that has "scope" throughout the task in which it is defined. Such task-dependent variables would provide a mechanism for re-establishing unfinished tasks at an appropriate juncture in the dialogue.

The design of the electronic mail front-end made extensive use of heuristics. These controlled the enabling and disabling of interface features, based on inferred knowledge of user experience and performance. The effects of these heuristics ranged from changing the level of help to controlling when and how uncompleted tasks would be suspended and re-established. Unfortunately CLG was unable to provide the dynamic specification required by the heuristics. Its notation does not provide slots for heuristics at the SEMANTIC level and the notation is not easily extended to cater for simultaneously described but mutually exclusive interface designs at the SYNTACTIC and INTERACTION levels. The interface selected for the user would be a result of "firing" or "not firing" of heuristics at the SEMANTIC level. This inadequacy of CLG is solely a result of it being used for something it was not designed to cope with, adaptive interface design. Nonetheless, it should be possible to extend CLG so that heuristics can be specified at the SEMANTIC level and associated with flags for use at the lower levels of description.

Other task analysis notations include Reisner's (1981) action grammars and Payne's (1984) task-action grammars (TAG). Both of these are based on syntactic descriptions in which tasks are rewritten into primitive operations. For adaptive interfaces it is necessary to consider the reverse mapping. To quote, Hoppe (1988),

> "Diagnosing the current task context for adaptation purposes requires the inverse mapping from internal tasks or primitive operations onto external tasks. In other words: it should be possible to use a task grammar also for parsing input sequences, thus facilitating the recognition of higher level task units."

Hoppe describes a bi-levelled task representation similar to TAG. The elementary task level concerns the primitive operations from which more complex tasks may be constructed. For instance, the elementary tasks "delete" and "move" can be combined to support a "replace" task. Elementary and composite tasks are each described as sets of pairs which consist of a symbolic feature name and a value. The transformation of composite tasks into a sequence of input primitives is described using re-write rules.

This formalism is referred to as LEXITAS, Language for EXternal Internal TAsk Specification. The formalism can be used to describe different ways of completing the same task. Composite tasks can be hierarchically described such that different levels of abstraction can be supported. However the notation still lacks the ability to describe either the circumstances under which one task method would be chosen in favour of another or points in the dialogue where it might be pertinent to offer adaptive features (for instance, help at an intra-task level).

Smolensky *et al.* (1984) concentrated on the documentation of task attributes as a focal point for task support. For the domain of creating hardcopy material, specifically using UNIX, a set of task attributes were derived using a number of techniques. The main conclusion of this study was that users could make use of task attributes in order to describe tasks. The implication being that attribute-oriented interactive environments could be provided. Put simply, such an environment would accept values for attributes from a user and the computer would be responsible for performing the necessary actions. Missing values would be requested by the system or generated as defaults.

Task Analysis for Knowledge Descriptions (TAKD) as proposed by Johnson (1985) is based on a form of notation for task description called Knowledge Representation Grammar (KRG). This notation was originally developed to describe training requirements. TAKD is well suited to interface design, particularly in highlighting the functions and facilities that will be required.

Johnson proposes a possible relationship between task analysis and the design of the interface as shown in Fig. 4.5. The Generalised

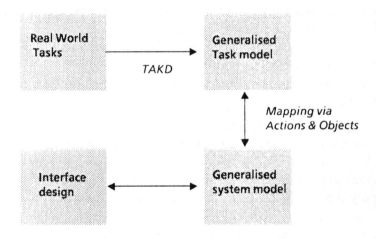

Fig. 4.5 User Interface design and TAKD.

Task Model (GTM) is based on descriptions of real world tasks and is the output of TAKD.

The first pass of the analysis is to take the results of the task analysis method, usually interviews, and group these by their subject matter. Following this, all the actions and objects listed are extracted resulting in a list of the form:

Validate/User Model/(with the) User/(using) paper/(using) flipchart/(using) voice.

The next stage is to iterate through those sentences a number of times, substituting where possible, generic actions and objects and ordering them in the form of KRG sentences. These sentences take the form of a generic action followed by one or more generic object phrases. For example, the sentence shown above could be reduced to:

Validate/User Model/(with) Expert/(using) Media

Johnson suggests that next, the attributes of each generic action and object should be defined.

A completed task analysis consists of: a series of KRG sentences, a list of all generic actions and the objects they influence, and a list of all generic objects and their attributes. The major difficulty encountered with TAKD, as a basis for modelling tasks to be supported by adaptive systems, is its reductionist approach. Rather than acknowledging user variability and modelling it, TAKD encourages the analyst to collapse across tasks as far as possible. Again this is not a criticism of TAKD because it was not developed as a technique to support the building of adaptive systems, we are simply pointing out its deficiencies in respect of adaptive system building.

In general the task analysis notations available at present simply do not possess adequate constructs for the description of alternative task methods. For instance, one user may prefer to supply parameters followed by commands while a second may prefer to supply commands then parameters. Modelling such alternatives can be quite lengthy with existing task notations, especially when the choice of one over another may depend on the previously executed task. Taking another simple example; unsolicited help. The contents of the help message may depend on the previous tasks completed and the predicted goals of the user. In such instances the task notation should ideally be able to describe the interplay between tasks and the consequent dialogue dependencies.

Another problem is that adaptive systems behave under the constraints imposed by modelled user characteristics as well as dialogue contexts. There is no provision in any of the task notations to show or model the interplay between these two determinants of adaptive behaviour at the design stage. In effect this places the burden on implementors and does not facilitate the identification of task related adaptations.

Task Model Implementations.

Implementations of task models can be as varied as the software environments, hardware availability, and uses to which they are put. During the early work on the AID project a task model was built using state transition networks. Such diagrams provide explicit descriptions of the sequencing in a communications process. When applied to interfaces, user actions are interpreted as state transitions.

Such specifications are also modular and easily modifiable. Furthermore, when state transition networks are automated to include calls to routines written in high-level languages and scripts for interrogating data structures, they can provide powerful prototyping tools and user interface management systems. RApid Prototyping of Interactive Dialogues (RAPID, Wasserman & Shewmake, 1984) is based on augmented state transition networks and was found to be a suitable vehicle for implementing the dialogue component of AID's front-end to an electronic mail system. From the task analysis documented using CLG an implementation was produced using RAPID.

The different networks represented different tasks and alternative routes through the network represented alternative means of accomplishing the same task or means of handling exceptions. At an intratask level, the transitions between subnetworks in the implementation, calls were made to the user-modelling component of the system informing it of the tasks completed and providing opportunities for adaptations to be made. For instance, the successful completion of a number of tasks resulted in the "level" of help on offer to a user being reduced. The development of the RAPID networks was relatively straightforward from the CLG specification, as Moran suggests it should be. Nonetheless, the point made earlier that it is difficult to provide intertask adaptations was found to be true in practice.

Hoppe (1988), in endeavouring to provide a means of identifying tasks in order to provide guidance on more optimal means of accomplishing the same task used a quite different task model implementation. The implementation was entirely in Prolog with all tasks represented as facts and rules in a Prolog database.

The work of Rouse *et al.* (1987) on providing support systems for operators of complex systems -- such as those for fighter pilot support and in process control -- uses a highly knowledge based approach to task modelling and performance modelling. Their "conceptual" system provides information management, error monitoring and adaptive aiding. Underlying this functionality is an operator model that assesses operator's activities, awareness, performance, resources and intentions. Their system identifies current tasks and predicts upcoming tasks using information about the operator state, system state and world state. In addition, tasks are dynamically classified as to whether they can be acomplished by human only, computer only, or are requiring of both human and computer. Tasks are also classified as to whether they are competing or complementary. Given the diversity of sources that can help in the identification and prediction of tasks it makes sense in the domain being considered to use a knowledge based approach. Of particular interest in this work is the extra overhead that the particular domain places on task modelling. For instance, the classification of tasks as to "who" can accomplish them. These type of requirements need not be considered in most domains but this work does demonstrate how very complex task modelling can become.

A Task Analysis Support Tool - TDL

Early work on the project based on the use of Command Language Grammar (CLG) as an approach to task analysis identified the value of employing a systematic approach to this aspect of formulating system requirements. However the inherent difficulties of deploying a "paper-based" methodology were also all too evident. Even for a rudimentary electronic mail system the volume of paperwork generated became unwieldy. This made it difficult to work collectively on the CLG specifications and, more importantly, gave rise to considerable effort in making revisions and amendments as the work progressed. This inhibited the essentially iterative processes associated with design. As a result it was felt appropriate to consider the development of a software based support tool for task analysis. One which reflected the staged approach to design embodied in CLG and in addition permitted the easy manipulation and refinement of design deliverables.

The essential philosophy of CLG has been retained, namely:

- that design originates from the user's perspective of requirements;

- that it should be dealt with in a series of stages;

- that the development of a "method" should be its outcome.

The principle objectives for this software tool were to provide facilities for:

- The identification and definition of task/system entities.

- The development and progressive refinement of task methods - including the definition of multiple methods in relation to adaptive systems.

- The cross checking and cross mapping of entities, methods and operations.

- The generalisation of operations and partial methods to evolve and encourage the formulation of common and reusable specifications.

The first stage in the use of the software tool is the definition of a "task tree", representing the task structure. Each node of the task tree has associated with it a method definition which is progressively extended. Initially this process starts with the inclusion of a narrative description of the task, leading to the definition of objects at the TASK level. Then, through the definition of operations associated with these objects, the provision of an outline method. And finally a procedural definition for the method is supplied.

It became evident that while the development of the TASK level could be separated out as a discrete design activity, the development of a more detailed method for each task is not constrained simply to consideration of the semantic/syntactic levels of CLG. The provision of an adequate and suitably complete METHOD demands additional levels of decomposition than the simple mappings between these levels of description. Accordingly, in TDL, the development of methods is taken as the declaration of operations for the objects defined in the task narrative (OUTLINE), followed by a more detailed definition of each of these as pseudo-code (METHOD). It is accepted that these definitions may well depend on the identification of objects and operations which are subordinate to and derived from aspects of previously defined objects and operations. The definition and manipulation of object and operation definitions has assumed a significance not evident in CLG and is supported through:

- *The provision of checks* - e.g. ensuring that each object defined in a task narrative has been associated with an operation in the task outline before progressing to the definition of a task method.

- *Cross referencing* between objects, operations and tasks.

- *The automatic referencing* of predefined operations and objects in the development of the various stages of task definition - e.g. the automatic highlighting of predefined objects in the development of a task description

- *Association of operations* with the task tree structure, enabling the designer to be prompted as to their availability - local to the task, task group or the entire system - when working on a particular task method.

The implementation of TDL displays separate windows, with full editing facilities, for the task tree, objects and operations. The selection of a node on the task tree will also open an additional window, giving a template for the development of the design detail. Similarly, the object and operation windows are supported by different template formats depending on the function being carried out. The system supports the simultaneous display and use of multiple windows, which can be configured according to the task the designer is currently working on. In the development of the object list or task outlines, for example, it may be appropriate to display only the task tree structure with a number of task node windows while the object and operation windows are closed. While during the development of task methods, it may be the task tree, the object list, a specific task node and the details of operations which are required. This flexibility supports the iterations that may take place in design, and the consequent changes to definitions that may be required.

TDL was applied retrospectively to the development of the phase 1 exemplar of the project, and two stages in this development are shown. The first display (Fig. 4.6) shows four active areas: the task tree, the current set of defined operations, the current set of defined

operation list

domi - confirm-removal
domi - delete
domi - identify-message
domi - identify-user
domi - read
domi - retrieve-message
domi - search
domi - send
domi - show
domi - specify

Operation Hierarchy
There are 2 references to identify-user......

send-message
  compose-or-retrieve-message
    compose-message
    retrieve-message
  check
  identify-user
    show
    search

object list

Display-area
helps
mailbox
message
Message-Display-area
message-recipient

object name: message
Description:
  A readable message which can be sent or received.
A message summary is comprised of the header and message status,
A list of messages represents a mailbox.

-Attributes-	
Body	Contains To ; From; Date;
Header	Time; Subject,
ID	
Number	
Status	

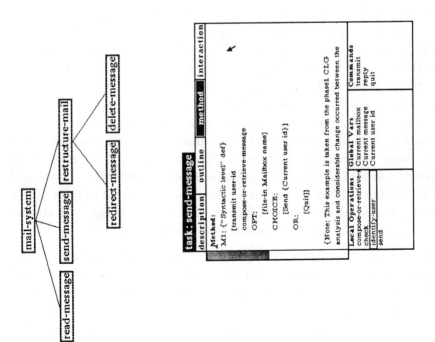

mail-system
read-message   send-message   restructure-mail
redirect-message   delete-message

task: send-message

description | outline | **method** | interaction

Method:
M1: {"Syntactic level" def}
  [transmit user-id
  compose-or-retrieve-message
  OPT:
    [file-in Mailbox name]
  CHOICE:
    [Send {Current user id}]
  OR:
    [Quit]]

{Note: This example is taken from the phase1 CLG analysis and considerable change occurred between the

Local Operations	Global Vars	Commands
compose-or-retrieve-	Current mailbox	transmit
check	Current message	reply
identify-user	Current user id	quit
send		

Fig. 4.6 TDL - 1.

objects and the method for the task "send message". The operation and object lists are both shown with a specific entry selected, particular details concerning each of these are shown in the lower part of the respective windows. Figure 4.7 shows the operation window now used to display the full list of operations. Two separate task windows are shown - the one for "send message" which displays the outline for that task, and the other for "read message" which shows two alternative methods that have been identified (i.e. candidates for adapation). The remaining window shows details for "mail system" - the highest level item on the task tree. It has been declared as an "organiser" node in order to include details of "generalised" operations that may be inherited by lower level tasks and which will be displayed automatically in task windows for lower level tasks as either "imported operations" or "commands". It should be noted that the status of operations can be changed as the design progresses. So that "reply", for example, may have been firstly defined as an operation and then declared as a global operation within an organiser node as its common usage became evident or it could have formed part of a predefined set of common operations declared before the detailed design commenced. It is thus possible to adopt various strategies during design. Either working from a simple narrative description of user requirements and progressively moving toward a detailed level of description. Alternatively, starting with objects/operation definitions - which have been identified either from previous designs, by other designers or arising from the designer's "bottom up" analysis - and ending with the integration of these definitions into the task methods. The designer is also able to employ both these approaches either in combination, or separately to different parts of the design. The minimum requirement to proceed with a design in TDL is to name either operations, objects or tasks. The sequence of the development of detail remains, with the exception of minor checks, a matter of preference.

The system is capable of being extended to include the specification of interaction methods, although the basis for the definition of generalisable "interaction rules" in the manner of CLG has yet to be settled for TDL. In view of developments in interface design it is likely that such rules will be predefined rather than arise as requirements from the details of a specific application. (In such circumstances the designer will be more concerned to review the

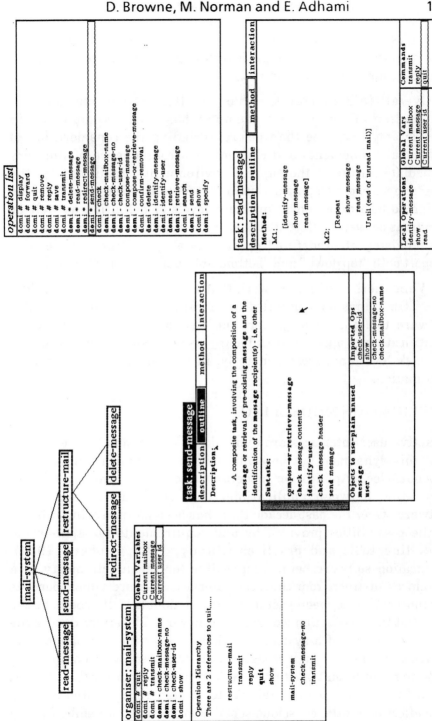

Fig. 4.7 TDL - 2.

dynamics of users interacting with the proposed system, an activity that may well best be accomplished through the deployment of some form of prototyping environment.)

Overall this support tool has fulfilled its expectations. A redefinition of the phase 1 exemplar has been accomplished in considerably less time than before, including the consideration of additional refinements and changes as a consequence of the very immediate nature of the support environment. Additionally, the consequence of developing a system that permits different parts of the design to be worked on at different levels of definition as well as iterations between different stages of the design process and includes the provision of predefined operations and entities, has been to support both "top down" and "bottom up" approaches to design.

While there is still more work that needs to be done, we consider that TDL stands as a useful demonstration of the framework of a software tool that can support the designer, particularly in the identification of opportunities for the use of adaptive techniques at the task level and, more generally, in the management of design information.

APPLICATION MODELLING

Adaptive user interfaces are dynamic by design and it is essential that this dynamism not be compromised by application software dependencies. Application modelling attempts to provide a clean separation between applications software and user interface software. Over the past decade there has been an increasing interest in the possibilities provided by and requirements for application modelling tools and practices (Bundy, 1984; Probert, 1984). Application software being responsible for the functionality of a system as distinct from the user interface software which permits communication between user and this functionality. It used to be the case that this distinction was rarely or never made, either during the design or coding of a system. To the end-user the distinction is of course transparent. An increased awareness of software engineering and the benefits that good practices can bring are one influence that has led to software being implemented in a more structured fashion. One effect being the conscious separation, rather than embellishing of user interface software. Given that as much as 40% of code may be for user interface purposes and that a large percentage of all maintenance is purely for user interfacing requirements, major savings can be gained. Thus there are good reasons, on purely system development and maintenance bases, why separation is a good practice. Two further reasons are likely to lead to separation being both the norm and an issue which warrants significant research.

At present, there are thousands of applications running on mainframe computers with user interfaces being supported in a transaction prossessing style on dumb terminals. With the proliferation of Personal Computers (PCs) there is now a large market for the user interfaces to mainframe applications to be provided on PCs. A PC-based interface would enable individuals to have more useable interfaces to existing applications in a style that is consistent with other applications running locally on their PC. All the user's interactive tasks will be supported from a single terminal. This requires software that can both mimic a transaction processing session and permit a new, and hopefully better, user interface to be added. Such software may be referred to as an application modeller. It must contain a model, implicitly or explicitly, of the application or at the very least a protocol for communicating with the application.

Another major reason why separation is likely to become the norm is the increasing sophistication of User Interface Management Systems. Such systems provide facilities for the prototyping and development of user interfaces. To achieve this, each provides mechanisms for communication with applications software. These mechanisms are commonly external function calls to the application which are embedded at suitable points in the dialogue structure. These context sensitive calls represent an implicit model of the application software. Unfortunately, the implicit nature of the model renders it difficult to ascertain what model of the application is being used and how it should be modified if the application software changes. This hinders the attainment of the benefits, particularly during maintenance, that are to be obtained through "clean" separation. Nonetheless, it is likely that UIMS will improve and with this improvement will come better application modelling facilities.

In one of the early and much cited descriptions of the requirements to be fulfilled by any UIMS the need for an application modeller was clearly recognised (Green, 1984). Unfortunately, the nature of such a modeller and what its functionality should be is not so clear. According to Green the design of the application model should be based upon the user's view of the semantics of the application. Within this perspective such a model would include significant aspects of a user model. Alty and McKell (1986) prefer to distinguish user model and applications model. In their view, the application model has two major roles:

- as a custodian of input integrity for the Application;

- as a source of advice and guidance to the User Model.

Such an application model would analyse user input and refer problems back to the user model. Such problems would be founded on consideration of the Application Model as drawing an 'expert' view of the application. Another perspective (Adhami and Browne, 1987) suggests that an application modeller can provide a basis for providing generic user interfaces to numerous applications of similar functionality. They suggest, for instance, that an application modeller could provide one interface across a finite set of electronic mail systems. The modeller would have a knowledge base for each mail system permitting messages to be directed by whichever one was most appropriate. Given that many users are unlikely to be concerned whether a message is routed via one mail system or another, this would seem a valuable proposition.

Thus application modellers are loosely defined in terms of the functionality that is expected of them. What can be generalised is the assertion that application modelling is a means by which user interface software can be separated from application software. The advantages of separation are identified by Adhami & Browne, (1987):

"Early prototyping of the user interface
Early prototyping is a powerful means of evaluating design decisions before they are implemented on the target system. Separation allows user interface prototyping tools to be used to evaluate important aspects of the interface without waiting for the application to be built.

Multiple interfaces to a single application
The requirements of different users within an organisation, using interactive computer systems, vary considerably. Separation enables different styles of user interface, tailored for different groups of users, to be developed for a single application. For instance, one style of

interface might be provided for novice users and a different style for experienced users. Alternatively, a menu driven interface and a command driven interface might be provided as options to the same applications software.

Generic interfaces to multiple applications

A further possibility, and a particularly interesting one, is the provision of a generic user interface to a number of applications with similar functionality. There are many organisations in which users need to access a number of similar computerised systems for information retrieval and computation. A major overhead in such organisations is the need for users to learn a range of interaction protocols for each system. Separation provides a real opportunity to develop consistent interfaces to a number of functionally similar applications. Generic interfaces can reduce the overheads of training and can increase productivity.

Maintenance and future modification

Separation of the user interface from the application software can play an important role in reducing maintenance costs. A considerable number of changes requested by users, after system installation, are concerned with the user interface. These changes are far easier to implement if the user interface is not embedded in the application code. This is particularly true at the early stages of a system's life and when new procedures are introduced into the user's organisation that affect the user interface. Furthermore, changes to the application software which do not affect the user interface can be implemented with greater ease. "

If one is concerned with building adaptive user interfaces then separation will be a "must", in all but the simplest of systems.

AN EXAMPLE OF AN APPLICATION MODELLER

The role of the application modeller or application expert (AE) in the phase one AID system was to provide a total separation between the processes dealing with the user interface and those primarily concerned with the application software. The user interface was developed for an electronic mail system, Telecom Gold, which had an existing user interface. Telecom Gold (TGOLD) resides on a remote host and therefore all communication was via a telephone line using a modem. Therefore it was necessary for the application modeller to make these aspects transparent to the the user interface software and invisible to users. The objectives which guided the specification of the AE were to :

(1) *Provide a mapping of user commands onto a set of appropriate TGOLD commands and identify problems during their execution.*

(2) *Analyse user commands in order to identify semantic errors before submitting "jobs"to the application software.*

(3) *Maintain communication with TGOLD and hide from the user those problems which are not related to the tasks being performed.*

(4) *Free the user interface from the specifics of TGOLD, because we were developing a generic interface suitable for any electronic mail system and not necessarily to TGOLD.*

In addition to these objectives, we wanted to investigate the feasibility of developing an application-independent architecture that could be utilised in the context of other applications.

A prerequisite to the design of the AE was the identification and formal description of the user's model of electronic mail at a task level. An analysis of electronic mail was performed (Browne *et al.*, 1986) using the Command Language Grammar (CLG) notation (Moran, 1981). This analysis provided the minimum set of entities and operations required by a user to accomplish electronic mail tasks. Entities identified included "letters" and "folders", and operations included "show a letter" and "forward a letter". The specification of objects to be returned to the Dialogue Controller was derived from the semantic level description of entities given by the CLG analysis. Error diagnostics were derived from the capability of the AE to perform semantic checks.

The next stage of development concentrated on producing a model of the electronic mail system. This was derived from the available reference and user manuals in conjunction with experimentation with the live system. This model represented:

- *the ordering and structure of the electronic mail commands;*

- *the functionality of each of the commands;*

- *the side-effects of commands and their reversibility;*

- *possible problems and recovery strategies;*

- *diagnostic messages and their meanings;*

- *default strategies taken by the application.*

Having produced the user task model and the application model it was necessary to specify the mapping between them. It should be noted that the user task model was derived without recourse to the particular electronic mail system. In principle the system could have been any one of a number of mail systems, provided that it supported the functionality required by the user tasks. In fact, the mapping between the two models showed that it was not possible to support directly the task of creating a new, but empty, mail folder. The need for this task was highlighted by the CLG analysis and it was felt that it should be supported for the purpose of preserving coherent structures (Carroll & Thomas, 1980). If users are allowed to delete empty mail-folders, then they should also be permitted to create empty mail-folders. In order to support this task, the AE had to use its model of the application system to combine commands in an appropriate sequence to produce the required result.

The Architecture of the Application Modeller.

A number of requirements guided the architectural design of the AE and the software approach to implementing the system. These included:

- The ability to make the representation of the models easily modifiable and comprehensible. This requirement arises because of the possibility that either model might be found to be inaccurate or that modifications are made to the application system. Such modifications were a distinct possibility with the particular electronic mail system being front-ended.

- The architecture needed to be generalisable so that it could act as a research vehicle for work in other application domains.

- The ability to reverse the effects of sequences of commands and parameters submitted to the application.

- The ability to return the application to a known state if something happens unexpectedly.

- The ability to interpret, and to reason about, the errors and warnings that the application provides.

A knowledge-based system approach was considered the most appropriate means for supporting these requirements. This was based on the following criteria:

- The declarative representation employed in knowledge based systems aids understanding of the models and eases their maintenance.

- Separation of the knowledge bases and the inference mechanism allowed the design of an architecture which could later be developed into a tool for application modelling.

- The declarative representations of the models in the AE could enable the symbolic simulation of the back-end application, allowing the evaluation of the user interface without the application.

- Separation of the knowledge bases and the inference mechanism provided the opportunity to replace the model of the TGOLD system with one for another mail system.

In addition, it was felt that the use of an Artificial Intelligence Programming environment would ease the effort of prototyping. The Poplog environment (Sloman, 1983) was chosen due to the multi-language programming facilities it provides. The architecture of the AE is illustrated in Fig. 4.8.

Knowledge Base One
This knowledge base (KB1) held the user task model and the application software specification, with the appropriate mappings between the two models. This mapping was coded declaratively in first order predicate logic. Thus, KB1 was responsible for the synthesis of user tasks into sequences of application software commands and arguments.

Knowledge Base Two
This knowledge base (KB2) contained a functional description of the application software's interface. This was represented as a state

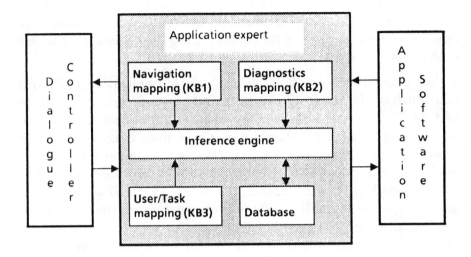

Fig. 4.8 Architecture of the Application Expert.

transition network with nodes representing states of the application software and arcs representing commands causing state to state transition. This representation was coded in first-order predicate logic. It was the responsibility of this knowledge base to provide mechanisms for returning the application software to a desirable state if the unexpected should happen. KB2 held knowledge about every state the application software could assume and described how to move from each of these states to every other state. This was an extremely powerful facility given that communications were via noisy telephone lines.

Knowledge Base Three
This knowledge base (KB3) held a specification of all the errors that might be identified by the AE, for particular user tasks. It also held a specification of how such errors should be reported to the dialogue controller. KB3 was implemented as a set of production rules.

Inference Engine
The inference engine employed a forward-chaining search strategy. Whenever a user request was to be submitted to the application, the inference engine was responsible for its processing. This processing

included semantic verification, mapping to TGOLD functions, submission to TGOLD, and verifying the logical consistency of the resulting output and reformatting it for the Dialogue Controller. The inference engine performed these tasks using the models represented in the knowledge bases.

The next major decision in the design of the application model was how much of the integrity checking and error correction should be performed by the AE without recourse to the application software. It was decided that the AE should perform as much diagnosis work as possible so that the user tasks performed during a session could be used to provide a more comprehensive set of error diagnostics than TGOLD provides. For this reason, the AE held a model of the current state of the user's mailbox. This included information about the user's mailboxes, their contents, the senders of messages and the identifiers for recipients of messages. During a single session, the database was updated to reflect the operations performed by the application software on behalf of the user. For instance, if a user deleted a message from a mailbox and later in the session attempted to read that message, the AE diagnosed that the user was attempting to read a deleted message. The application software would only have been able to report that the message did not exist.

The Operation of the Application Expert.
Syntax Checking
All syntax checking was performed by the Dialogue Controller. In an adaptive system, such checks cannot be the responsibility of the AE. The reason for this is that the dialogue controller, in combination with the user model may be offering the user many syntactically different options. The AE therefore assumed syntactic correctness of the user tasks submitted to it by the Dialogue Controller.

Semantic Checking
Although the user commands received by the AE are syntactically correct, they could be semantically wrong. The AE therefore performs semantic checks on user commands before synthesising them and submitting them to the application software. Three types of semantic error were detected by the AE. The first relates to references made to non-existent entities. For example, this could occur if the user attempted to send a message to a recipient who is not

known to the system. Alternatively, the user might try to create an entity, such as a mail folder, which already exists. The second category of errors were caused by illegal operations on entities. For example if the user requested that a mail item be filed in the folder "intray", this indicated that the user might not fully understand the concept of "intray". The identification of such errors by the AE allowed the Dialogue Controller to provide appropriate guidance to the user. Finally there were commands which were semantically meaningless. For example the user might have specified that a mail item in folder "x" should be filed in folder "x". As far as the application software was concerned this command could be processed but would not change the state of the user's mailbox and hence was unnecessary. The AE identified such cases and reported them to the Dialogue Controller.

Synthesis of Tasks

Having performed semantic checks on the user commands, the AE retrieved from KB1 the necessary tokens to be submitted to the application. If the application software was not in the appropriate state to receive the tokens, KB2 was accessed to obtain another set of tokens that would take the application to the necessary state. Having achieved the appropriate state, the tokens required to perform the user task were submitted to the application software. Having submitted tokens to the application software it was essential to check that the task had been performed accurately. Firstly, the expected final state of the system was obtained from KB2 and checked against the actual state of the application software and secondly the result of each operation was checked. For instance, if an operation should erase an existing message and leave the system at a "mail prompt" then this was checked. If these checks indicated that the application software did not process the tokens as expected then the AE would pass further tokens to the application software to achieve the appropriate state and affect the appropriate operations.

As an example of the power of the AE to maintain the integrity of its model of the application data structure, consider the user task of "reading the third as yet unread message in a mailbox". On submitting this task to the application software it was possible that, due to line noise, the application would identify the correct message but fail to pass this message to the AE. As a side-effect this message would assume the status of being "read" as opposed to "unread". If the same user task were now submitted to the application, what was originally the fourth unread message would now be returned to the application expert. To avoid such occurrences the AE always checked the outcome of the application processing. In this particular example, the AE would have replaced the user task with a semantically different task that had the desired outcome. Thus, the AE had the power to reverse undesired side-effects that occur in the application software.

Interpretation of Application Output

Results received from the application are parsed and returned to the Dialogue Controller once the user task had been accomplished successfully. The parsing performed by the AE enabled the dialogue controller to present output in alternative formats, sequences and amounts. For instance, the presentation of a message to one user might provide the message header and directly below it the first twenty lines of the body of the message, for a different user only ten lines of the body might be presented, freeing screen space for other prompts or helpful messages.

The Application Expert in Retrospect

The most significant contribution of the AE was that the phase 1 AID user interface was independent of the specific electronic mail application. Other contributions to the design process, the prototyping stage and the overall quality of the interface included :

- During the design stage, the CLG analysis provided a specification of the functionality of the application system from the user interface viewpoint. Once this functionality had been defined, the AE freed the dialogue designers from the details of TGOLD.

- During the prototyping stage, the AE provided a vehicle to symbolically simulate the behaviour of the application software in response to any user commands without any need to access TGOLD.

- The explicit and declarative representation of the user task model and the application model proved invaluable when later modifications and additions became necessary.

- The knowledge based approach resulted in an architecture which could not only be utilised to replace TGOLD with another electronic mail system, but could also be developed into a tool for application modelling.

In summary, the AE provided a productive agent for managing the communication between the two components of an interactive computer system. For many of the adaptive user interfaces that will be built in future years there will be a requirement for an application modeller. There is a significant market for new user interfaces to be built that run on personal computers and communicate with mainframe applications. If tools can be provided that render this "front ending" significantly easier than it is at present, then developers may consider the inclusion of adaptive user interfacing features as being desirable and practical. Application modellers have a major role to play because they can render the user interface significant independence from applications. This in turn would permit early prototyping, make maintenance easier and reduce the cost of supporting adaptation.

CONCLUSION

The reasons for providing adaptive interfaces were reviewed in Chapter 2 and some of the means for modelling these reasons were discussed here. One particular taxonomy of User Models, generated during the AID project, was used as the basis for discussion but any one of a number of alternative taxonomies could have been used. It is to be hoped that generalisable user modelling packages will become available in the fullness of time to facilitate this rather difficult element of adaptive system production.

Having established how user modelling might be undertaken we then proceeded to discuss the flexibility required at the user interface of adaptive systems and how this might be supported during specification and implementation. While it is not the case that any one notation or UIMS implementation can be recommended outright, the project's belief was that the event-based notation and supporting tools offered most flexibility.

Most adaptive systems will pose a requirement for task modelling. Available techniques were reviewed. The general conclusion is that there is a paucity of useful tools in this area. This inadequacy needs to be rectified, and not simply for the purposes of building adaptive systems. To this end a task modelling tool developed by the AID project was presented.

Finally, an architecture for the separation of user interface and application software was presented. Given the benefits that such a separation can afford and the lack of other examples, it was felt worthwhile to devote a significant portion of this chapter to the topic.

Research into adaptive systems would benefit greatly from further advances in all four of the areas discussed above. Without such advances the provision of adaptive user interfaces will be uneccesarily costly for most commercial applications.

Chapter 5
Adaptive Interface Techniques

P. Totterdell, P. Rautenbach, A. Wilkinson and S. O. Anderson

In this chapter we will examine some of the techniques which can be applied to the development of adaptive computer interfaces. And where appropriate describe how the techniques have been demonstrated by exemplar systems produced by the AID project (cf. Rautenbach et al, 1988) First, we examine how the exemplars developed on the AID project conform to a general architecture for adaptive interfaces. Then look at different types of adaptive interface technique and finally at a number of key human computer interaction issues relating to these techniques.

The AID project investigated a range of techniques for developing adaptive interfaces. In Chapter 3 we described a two-level architecture for adaptive interfaces and here we begin our account of adaptive interface techniques by illustrating how three of the exemplars developed on the project conform to that architecture. It is interesting to note that only the third of the exemplars was built with the foresight of the architecture; giving us added confidence in the generality of the structure.

ARCHITECTURE FOR ADAPTATION

To recap on the two level architecture, it should be recalled that the higher level adaptor evaluates the performance of the alternative lower level theories by monitoring the interaction cues at the interface. The best lower level theory is then chosen on the basis of the performance metrics. In some of the examples the reader may prefer to see the lower level as "controlling" rather than "adapting" the interface. The two level architecture is nonetheless appropriate because the higher level is adapting the way the lower level controls the interface for the current situation, and does this by evaluating the relative success of the alternative control strategies in satisfying the objective.

A Self-regulating Adaptive Interface to a Telephone Directory.

Greenberg and Witten (1985) built an adaptive menu interface to a telephone directory. The adaptor in this interface modelled the relative frequencies with which each name in the directory was accessed by a particular user and adapted the menu tree so that each menu option had an approximately equal probability of being selected. This put more frequently accessed items higher in the menu tree and hence reduced the mean number of menu selections required to access an item.

This first level of adaptive architecture was able to adapt the structure of the menu tree to suit an individual user's need to access particular telephone numbers, as long as this followed a Zipf distribution (Zipf, 1949). Trevellyan and Browne (1987) replicated the system for the AID project and added a second level adaptor to assess the success of the first level adaptor. This second level of architecture monitored the menu interactions to see how the average depth of menu selection changed over time. If the adaptation was working, the average depth of selection required could be expected to decrease to a stable minimum as the interface adapted to the particular mix of names accessed by the user.

If, however, the depth increased with time, the second level concluded that adapting the menu tree according to a Zipf distribution was inappropriate for this user and so substituted a flat distribution; this had the effect of keeping the menu tree static. The theory was that if the user's accesses were not following a Zipf distribution it would be more appropriate to stop changing the menu tree and so allow the user to learn the sequence of selections for a given name in the menu, that is to allow the user to adapt to the menus. (Fig. 5.1).

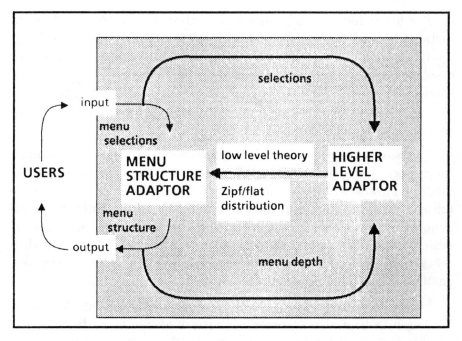

Fig. 5.1 Adaptive telephone directory generalised architecture.

Adaptive Spelling Corrector

The adaptive spelling corrector was based on work by Damereau (1964) which accounted for most misspellings using the following four rules:

MISSPELLING	RULE	CORRECTION
missing letter	M	*add missing letter*
extra letter	E	*remove extra letter*
wrong letter	W	*replace wrong letter*
transposed adjacent letters	T	*swap transposed letters*

The lower level adaptor detected a misspelt word (one not in its dictionary) and generated a list of possible correctly spelt words by applying each of the four rules in turn. Thus the correction list displayed to the user was intended to be "adapted" to the user's immediate need to correct the current misspelling and the user was able to select the correctly spelt word. The correction process then moved on to the next misspelt word.

The role of the second level adaptor was to arrange the words in the correction list with the most likely near the top. This was done by monitoring which rules accounted most often for the user's particular misspellings and applying the rules in order of applicability when generating the words in the correction list. That is, the order in which the rules were applied to generate the list of possible corrections was adapted by the second level to accord with the particular user's history of misspellings.

The relative frequencies of misspellings due to missing (M), extra (E), wrong (W) and transposed (T) letters was evident from which word in the correction list was selected by the user as the right word in each case, and noting which rule was responsible for this word being in the list.

The order in which these relative frequencies ranked the four rules was taken as characteristic of that particular user. That is, the rule order corresponding to the misspellings of a particular user acted

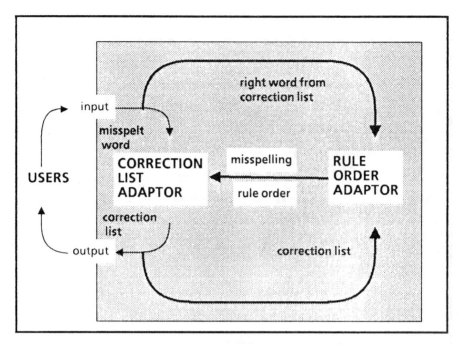

Fig. 5.2 Adaptive spelling corrector generalised architecture.

as the interface's model of that user, and determined for that user how near the top of the list words generated by each of the four rules appeared as candidate corrections.

For example, a user exhibiting mostly missing letters but more transposed letters than extra ones and very few wrong letter misspellings would be modelled as MTEW. For such a user, missing letter corrections would be listed at the top, followed by transposed, extra and finally wrong letter corrections. The rationale for this was that because the user finds most of his or her corrections near the top of the list, correcting misspellings will be made quicker for the user.

Adaptive Menu Defaults

The idea behind this interface was that menu operations could be speeded up by pre-positioning the mouse cursor at the user's most likely selection when the user pops up a menu. The generalised architecture is shown in Fig. 5.3.

To predict which option from a menu was likely to be the next one selected, the first-level adaptor used one of three rules; each rule

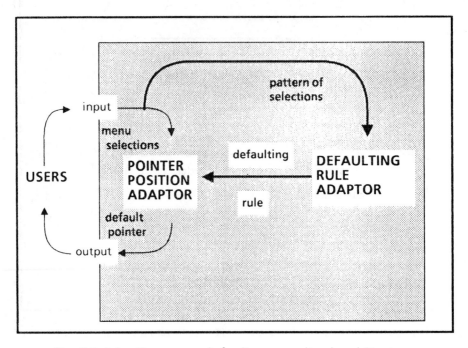

Fig. 5.3 Adaptive menu defaults generalised architecture.

corresponding to a characteristic pattern of menu use. For example, the "repetition" rule predicted that the next selection would be a repeat of the last and so positioned the cursor next to it. The alternation rule predicted the selection before last and the predominance rule predicted the most frequent selection. Each of these three rules used cues derived from the recent history of selections from the menu; specifically, the last selection, the selection before last and the most frequent selection.

The assumption behind adding a second level adaptor to the architecture is that no single rule can predict the next selection as successfully as a rule which uses the pattern of selections exhibited in the recent past to choose between the three rules already described. For example, if the second-level adaptor finds sequences of repeated selections in recent menu use then it will use this as a cue to adapt the first level adaptor to the repetition rule.

Note that, unlike the previous example, the theory was not suggesting that the pattern of menu use was characteristic of a given user but that the three different patterns of menu use might correspond to the menu being used by the user for different kinds of tasks. For example; a cut and paste menu might be used with repeated cut operations when shortening a document; alternation of cut and paste when rearranging a document; and a predominance of paste operations interspersed with cuts when duplicating sections of a document.

GENERAL ADAPTIVE INTERFACE TECHNIQUES

During the AID project a number of techniques were used in different forms in more than one adaptive interface. This section describes these commonly occurring techniques for supporting adaptive interfaces. We can distinguish roughly between these techniques by the sophistication of the underlying theory of the user embodied in the technique. In particular we distinguish three types of technique: the knowledge-independent approach of the genetic algorithm, the knowledge-impoverished or interactive approaches of scheduling and pattern matching, and the knowledge rich approaches of discourse modelling and user modelling.

Genetic Algorithms

As we saw in Chapter 3, the adaptation of a self-adapting interface to the changing needs of a user is analogous to the adaptation of life-forms to their environment through natural selection. In fact there are some machine learning algorithms that are modelled on an idealised version of the role of genetic inheritance within this evolutionary process; and these genetic algorithms are thought to constitute a potentially powerful domain independent strategy for achieving adaptive learning (Smith, 1984; Holland, 1984). It might therefore be worth considering the use of a genetic algorithm as the mechanism of adaptation for a self adapting interface.

The genetic algorithm paradigm essentially involves the cultivation of knowledge structures in competition with each other. A generation of knowledge structures is tested in its environment and ordered according to an evaluation of their relative performances. New structures are generated by combining previous structures on a probabilistic basis, favouring those that are known to be successful.

The new structures are then tested in the environment and the process repeats until an acceptable solution is discovered.

Powerful search performance has been demonstrated for learning systems containing knowledge structures representing: functional optimization of parameter values (DeJong, 1980), game-playing programs (Smith, 1984), competing sets of production rules (Forsyth, 1987), and competing decision rules within a classifier system (Holland, 1984).

The recombination of knowledge structures is achieved using genetic operators which loosely reflect the transformations made to genetic material, such as DNA, during reproduction. For example, the crossover operator takes two strings of information, removes a substring at random from one string and swaps it with the corresponding string in the other; thus a-b-c-d-e and v-w-x-y- z could become a-w-x-y-e and v-b-c-d-z. Other operators include mutation (the random alteration of part of a string) and inversion (the reversal of a random part of a string). Further artificial operators are also possible; for example, Wilson (1986) used an intersection operator which simply extracted elements that were common to both strings chosen for recombination, inserting non-specific pattern-matching elements in the gaps (so a-b-c-d-e and a-f-c-g-e might become a-*-c-*-e).

Genetic operator activity constrains the knowledge representation of the learning system being developed. Any domain knowledge initially available to the system must be represented with a structure that can be rearranged by the genetic operators. The representation must also facilitate the evolution of rules for manipulating the domain knowledge. Most attempts to use the paradigm have cultivated knowledge structures that are simple fixed-length binary codes which map onto the parameters or rules that constitute the domain space (Holland, 1984; Smith, 1984; Wilson, 1986). Alternatively, Forsyth (1987) has experimented with an evolutionary learning system that directly manipulated structures consisting of lists of parameters and parts of rules like Boolean operators. In each approach the genetic operators function without any regard for specific interpretation, so an ingenious syntax design is essential to ensure that structures can still be interpreted following recombination.

To the extent that genetic algorithms have been successfully used to cultivate knowledge bases in various other domains, the prospects for using the paradigm to develop a rule set that might support a self adapting interface would seem promising. The paradigm should also be well suited to cope with the dynamic nature of the dialogue which occurs because the user and system are continually adapting to each other.

There are, however, some grounds for caution: to date, successful implementations of genetic algorithms have needed a large number of generations of rule sets in order to evolve useful knowledge bases. Thus when Smith (1984) cultivated a knowledge base that could play poker very successfully, the evolution of the system involved 4000 cycles of generating competing knowledge bases, evaluating them, and recombining their knowledge structures to generate further knowledge bases for testing. In this example the poker playing prowess of each potential knowledge base was evaluated by playing the program against another poker playing program, and the whole evolution process was achieved in a short period of computer processing time. Similarly other systems have been developed in domains where the performance of competing knowledge structures could be evaluated using computerized training data (e.g. Forsyth, 1987).

For the purpose of implementing self adapting interfaces whose underlying rule sets are to be evaluated through direct interaction with the human user, such a long process of evolution would obviously be intolerable. Some research undertaken by Wilkinson (1987), in collaboration with the AID project, highlighted this particular weakness of the paradigm for implementing self adapting interfaces.

Wilkinson implemented a self adapting interface driven by a simple genetic algorithm which was designed to adapt the configuration of VDU attributes (for example, text font size, screen colour, and line spacing) to a particular user's preference during direct interaction with that user. The system exhibited powerful search performance, being able to converge on a target configuration of VDU attributes having tested on average only 0.2% of all possible configurations during computer based simulations of the adaptive process. However, this kind of performance would still have required a user to judge several hundred configurations of the interface before arriving at an acceptable configuration - obviously an unrealistic demand.

Although the paradigm may not provide a mechanism that can adapt a completely undifferentiated knowledge base during direct interaction with the human user, alternative uses of genetic algorithms for adaptive interfaces are more promising. Levine *et al.* (1986) successfully employed a genetic algorithm to optimize the design of individually customized interfaces and communication devices for disabled users. Instead of adapting the interface directly to the user, the user was represented by a computer-based model against which the genetic algorithm tested candidate solutions, thus enabling a large number of possible solutions to be evaluated without inconveniencing the user directly.

In fact, the user model that Levine *et al.* employed was based on the time taken to move to different parts of a keyboard, taking into account the distance and direction of movement; relatively simple, but apparently effective in the context. However, if other relevant aspects of the individual user could be modelled using a computer simulation then a genetic algorithm might be a good mechanism for adapting an interface to the model as a first step towards adaptation to the individual. The resulting knowledge base could then be refined through direct interaction with the user.

In conclusion, the genetic algorithm paradigm can deliver an effective adaptive mechanism, though it is doubtful that the mechanism will converge onto an acceptable solution rapidly enough for direct use with users. The successful application of the paradigm in other domains has required that competing rule sets are evaluated against computer based training data. The knowledge base underlying the self-adapting interface should therefore perhaps be developed using a computer-based model of the user, and then refined during direct interaction with that user.

Adaptive Scheduling

Adaptive scheduling was a common technique in AID exemplars. The order in which operations or subtasks are to be performed is often overspecified in interactive systems when it would be better to allow the order to adapt to suit the user or circumstances. Bennett (1976) makes the point that: "We can't build in process (a prescribed sequence of function use) because process is unknown in advance, changes over time for a user and often is different for a different user."

For example, when a user is writing a document the timing of the flagging of spelling errors depends on the user's preference and the nature of the writing task (e.g. type of document). In one circumstance it may be best to flag and correct spelling errors immediately as they are typed. In others it may be better to correct at the completion of each sentence or paragraph. Thus the sequence of editing and correcting operations may need to be adapted to circumstances.

One of the AID exemplars did just this (Friend, 1987). The timing of the flagging of spelling errors was adapted to suit the user's past history of spelling correction. If spelling errors were corrected by the user before going on to type the next word then future errors would be flagged immediately they occurred (i.e. at the word level). If errors were corrected after each sentence then they would be flagged at a sentence level. And if error correction was left until the end of a paragraph, future errors were flagged per paragraph.

Another example of a scheduling problem occurs in automated diary management and in particular setting a date for a meeting. The order in which participants are asked to confirm or suggest a date for a meeting can affect the number of failed attempts at setting the date, and hence the number of times a date is pencilled in by each participant. Typically, a secretary would know which people to ask first from past experience, probably those people with least flexibility to accommodate dates.

By recording which users are most often the cause of a meeting being rescheduled, the secretary's skill can be automated so that the order in which participants are consulted adapts to the relative availability of the participants. This is a particular case of exploring a multiple- constraint problem by first satisfying the most stringent constraints.

All examples of scheduling can be seen as choosing a particular sequence (or order) from the set of all possible sequences (or orderings). For adaptive interfaces, the possible sequences are the

user interface variants and in effect the adaptive mechanism chooses
one as being best adapted to the user's needs. However, the chosen
sequence will probably be adapted incrementally as the interaction
progresses rather than being explicitly selected from a library of
alternative sequences (i.e. interface variants).

Pattern Matching

The cues used in the adaptive menu defaults interface described
earlier in this chapter can be seen as patterns in user interaction.
One view of adaptive interfaces sees the adaptor as a pattern matcher
which tries to match the user's interactions to patterns which classify
such interactions as indicative of a need for one user interface variant
or another. Or put another way, the user's need for a particular
interface variant is recognised from a particular pattern of user
interaction.

An example of a system which uses one type of pattern match is
the Reference Information Provider (RIP) developed on the AID
project. RIP is an adaptive information support agent designed to
run concurrently with an editor. The system counts keywords in the
text being edited and checks for matches against entries in a
bibliography. If the number of matches reaches a prespecified limit,
the reference to the matching document is retrieved and displayed in
a scrollable window. Different text will trigger the retrieval of
different references. The system is adaptive since it embodies a
simple theory about how to tell if one document is relevant to
another. It would also be possible to adapt the relevance criteria.

Taking the adaptive menu defaults as another example, the need
for the menu to default to the last selection from the menu was
recognised from a particular pattern of recent menu use, e.g.

$$\ldots S S \ldots$$

This sequential pattern, or 'trace', may be read as 'any sequence of
selections, followed by (any) selection S, followed by (the same)
selection S, followed by any sequence of selections'. Thus, S can
match any actual selection from the menu as long as the same
selection occurs twice in succession. This pattern therefore
represents (or recognises) repetition of selections in menu use.

The pattern used to recognise alternation in the adaptive menu defaults example was:

$$\ldots S \_ S \ldots$$

which means "any sequence of selections, followed by any selection S, followed by any single selection, followed by the same selection S, followed by any sequence of selections". Note that this pattern not only recognises any two alternating selections but also any sequence where a particular selection occurs every other selection regardless of the selection in between. Thus true alternation is a special case of this where two such patterns involving different selections in place of S are interleaved, e.g.:

$$\ldots \text{cut paste cut paste} \ldots \quad \text{is an interleaving of}$$

$$\ldots S \_ S \ldots \quad \text{where S} = \text{cut, and}$$

$$\ldots S \_ S \ldots \quad \text{where S} = \text{paste}$$

The sequence . . . cut cut cut cut . . . is recognised by both the patterns for alternation and for repetition. In practice this "overlapping" of the cue for one rule with the cue for another did not matter, since both predicted the same next selection on long sequences; but it does question the need for having both where the alternation pattern on its own might suffice. In this case the advantage of the repetition pattern is that it can recognise repetition after the second occurrence of the same selection whereas the alternation pattern would only recognise it after the third occurrence. In general, there is only a problem when two patterns found in the same user interaction are cues for conflicting choices of interface (or theory) variant.

Simple traces such as these can be used to represent many patterns in the user's interactions at the interface but there are some "patterns" of interactions which simple traces cannot cope with. For example, recognising predominance of one selection in menu use; which is based on frequency of occurrence rather than particular juxtapositions of occurrences.

The advantage of using simple traces to represent cues for adaptive interfaces is that they can be implemented by simple template matching mechanisms operating on a simple record of the history of user interactions, and this record of history need only span the length of the longest pattern template. Thus, in the adaptive menu defaults example, a record of the current selection plus the last two selections was sufficient for matching the repetition and alternation templates.

In principle an adaptive interface can be based on pattern learning, rather than pattern matching, by enabling the adaptor to recognise for itself the patterns present in user interactions without these having to be predefined by the designer.

An example would be to enable the adaptor to recognise, by learning for itself, all sequences of length n which are followed by (and therefore predict) a given next element of the sequence. In the case of menu defaults this would allow the interface to learn those sequences which predict, as the next selection, each option in a menu (as long as the next selection was predictable from the previous n selections). Such a learning adaptor could simply learn by rote the actual sequences which most often precede a given menu selection and recognise these sequences as the cue to default to the given selection. It would be necessary to use techniques for inducing general patterns from specific ones. However, there are known techniques in this area (Michalski *et al.* 1986).

Moving on to the issue of the representation of patterns it is worth noting that the relationships between user interaction cues and user interface variant (or theory variant for a second level adaptor) can often be represented by rules of the form:

IF particular cue found THEN particular variant is appropriate

Such rules can then be used by an automated agent of change in the user interface. Given a rule for each variant, the adaptor would check for a rule whose condition is satisfied by recent user interactions and then make the corresponding choice of interface variant or theory variant. The set of rules thus represent the theory on which the adaptation is based, and it is a relatively easy matter to build a "table-driven", or generic, adaptor which can be parameterised by a particular set of rules in order to implement a particular theory. Changing the set of rules then corresponds directly to changing the theory to a different theory.

This was in fact the approach adopted for the adaptive menu defaults. A generic framework for a two-level adaptor was built and then populated with rules for adaptive defaulting. This allowed, for example, an alternation rule to be added after trying the interface out with only two rules, and this alternation rule to be changed relatively easily when a better implementation of it was found.

In principle, a single generic implementation of a two-level adaptor could have been implemented to support the three examples described earlier - the telephone directory access system, the spelling corrector, and the adaptive menu defaults. This way of building adaptive user interfaces would allow more than one adaptor in an interface to share the same program code, with a resultant saving in program size, time, etc.

Before we leave this section it is worth reporting the results of an experiment which attempted to adapt the user's interaction with a system by adapting the functioning of a mouse controller. The adaptive mouse technique was interesting because it attempted to recognise continuous rather than discrete patterns in the users interaction. Although the results were not encouraging, it is a good example of both the variety of options available to the interface designer and the way in which existing solutions are sometimes found to be sufficiently well adapted to make enhancements unnecessary.

It was originally ventured that by gathering information about the direction and speed of mouse movements it would be possible to infer the user's intentions with respect to selecting objects on the screen and that this information could be used to adapt the movement of the mouse in order to improve the user's operational speed and accuracy. In particular it was proposed that speed and accuracy would improve if the mouse movement was made faster in the direction in which the mouse was being moved over "open space" and then slowed down over the required selection.

The experiment required ten users to play a simple game in which they had to hit five targets highlighted at random on the screen. The measures were the user's subjective reaction, the average time per target selection and the number of overshoots (counted by observing a stepped replay of the user's trial). The users were given eight mouse strategies which varied speed, prediction (on or off) and deceleration near target (on or off). The results showed that the users preferred strategy was one which moved the mouse at three times the normal speed but decelerated near the target. The selection times were generally quicker when the system did not make prediction. Accuracy was best for the slower strategies.

The first conclusion was that it was difficult to predict the user's intentions without knowledge of both their interaction history and of objects on the screen. It was also noticed that experienced users commonly describe an arc with the mouse rather than a straight line, which confounded the prediction strategies. Also there is a very tight feedback loop between hand and eye and users did not take to this being disturbed. All very good reminders of the need for assumptions and metrics to be specified early in the design process.

Context

A well adapted interface shares with its users a compatible understanding of the situation in which interaction is taking place, and hence has the basis for a succinct dialogue which has the intended interpretation on both sides of the interface. We will call the situation in which an interaction takes place the "context" of that interaction. The full context of an interaction as seen by the user and as seen by the system will be very different. The user typically sees the interaction in a richer context including personal, work and social attributes. Communication takes place where system and user contexts overlap.

The same user input (or output) can have different interpretations in different contexts because the role of context is to provide the basis for appropriately interpreting what is said by adding what is implicit in the context. Thus establishing a context for interaction allows an "efficient" dialogue in which the minimum information needs to be said exchanged.

Assuming all user input is meaningful, an adaptive interface attempts to pick an appropriate interpretation from a number of plausible interpretations. Therefore, to make an adaptive interface we need to identify the different plausible interpretations and we need a notion of appropriateness. The adaptive interface attempts to interpret user input in context and reflects back to the user, in its choice of output, the context it is assuming. This establishes a shared context for interaction.

At a detailed level, the context changes from moment to moment as the user interacts with the system. Hence, there is a need for the system, and in particular the user interface, to track these changes in user context. Also, at a gross level, different users may imply different contexts and therefore a user interface may have to determine and then adapt to each user's individual needs.

In principle, every input from the user signals a change in circumstances and hence a possible cue to adapt to a new context. The change of context is obvious when the user presses a help function key. However it is less obvious, but nonetheless true, that every character entered into a word processor signals a change in context. From the system's viewpoint, these cases are equivalent in as much as they both demand a change in system state which is reflected in a change of appearance and/or behaviour at the user interface.

For the designer of an adaptive user interface (AUI), the problem is one of appropriately interpreting a user's input at any point in the interaction and establishing an appropriate context for interaction. Generally this requires defining and maintaining additional information to represent the context. The context is used in deciding on the appropriate interpretation for an interaction and in determining the next interaction. Thus, the designer must decide on the form of the context, how interaction changes and how the context influences interaction. One aim of an adaptive system is to provide more variability in the interpretation of user input in an attempt to make better use of the resources brought to the dialogue by the user.

In this section, condensed from Anderson (1987), we consider how to enhance the interaction language of systems via the introduction of context. In particular, we look at the increasingly sophisticated ways in which systems can utilise context, from systems which use simple indicators of context to those which transform context by altering the conditions for its interpretation.

In many conventional systems, the language of interaction is closely related to the basic operations associated with the *types* of objects being manipulated. Often the interface language is little more than a syntactic sugaring of the signature of the *types* used in the interface. User input is interpreted only as a direct command to modify or display some object in the system.

This situation may be a historical consequence of design work focussing on the design of *types*, i.e. the system functionality. Such design is highly result oriented, i.e. it only supports the transformation of those objects which will eventually be seen as the result of the interaction. Very little of the system's resources are devoted to keeping track of the context of the interaction. Yet Suchman (1987) has shown that understanding context is crucial to effective human computer interaction. However, the question is to what extent can systems make good use of context?

In simple command systems the meaning of each command is given as a state-to-state transition function. In giving such meaning definitions, the interface designer usually conforms to three important conventions:

- The definition depends only on the formal aspects of interaction, i.e. not on performance characteristics such as typing speed or hesitation.

- The meaning definition is context free in the sense that there is no notion of context over and above the current state.

- The definition of meaning is usually compositional in that the meaning of a compound command is given in terms of the meaning of its parts.

In attempting to construct adaptive systems we move away from these assumptions concerning the language of interaction. The usual strategy is to retain the formal context-free compositional semantics of commands as the core of the system but in addition to facilitate use of the system by interpreting the user's behaviour according to some hidden criteria. The characteristic of these criteria is that they often break with the conventional assumptions made about the interpretation of user input: they are often non-formal, using measures like timing and hesitation; they usually make use of some notion of context based on frequencies and distributions; and they are often non-compositional. The hidden criteria are used to decide on the appropriate interpretation for an interaction in order to improve the "efficiency" of communication. The additional information which results from the interpretation of the input is the "context" of the interaction.

Let us look in more detail at how we can use context to improve the efficiency of simple interface languages. First, consider the following sentence: "Bring me the end of year report." This sentence may be uttered by many different people in different circumstances. Barwise and Perry (1983) call such sentences efficient because they can sensibly be interpreted in many different contexts and they draw on contextual information to determine their interpretation. The interpretation of the sentence requires a narrow though useful class of contextual features, namely the indexicals.

The indexicals of an utterance are used to instantiate the demonstratives of a sentence with the appropriate object. For example in the sentence we considered above, "me" stands for the speaker (which varies depending on who the speaker is); and "end of year report" stands for one of a number of different documents (e.g. end of 1987, 1988, etc.) disambiguated by the context.

The hearer's resources are crucial in determining the indexicals of a sentence. In our example, if the hearer's idea of the speaker or the year of interest deviates from the speaker's idea then confusion results. For our example, both of the following interpretations are possible given different resources on the hearer's part:

(A) If the hearer has no idea of the location of the report but knows what end of year reports are then the hearer may initiate dialogue about the filing system for reports, however

(B If the hearer has no knowledge of end of year reports but knows the filing system then the hearer may initiate dialogue on the features of end of year reports pertinent to their filing.

Correctly tracking the indexicals in a language can greatly improve the quality of the interaction. In terms of a simple interface, this translates into the use of default parameters for commands. This involves constructing a context consisting of:

- A small number of standard names. In natural language these include *this, that, here, there.* In systems these could be: *default-read-file, default-help-file,* etc.

- A set of rules for associating system objects with these names.

  - An evaluation and selection of the rules based on performance
    comparisons.

A number of systems already embody the first two principles. For
example, editors usually maintain a notion of "here" as the current
position in text. Whenever a character is inserted the context is
appropriately updated and the display informs the user of the update.
If this was not true then whenever a user typed a new character they
would also be required to explicitly state the required position of the
character.

For an editor there is probably only one good rule of association
between the name "here" and the textual object. However, in
situations where there is more than one plausible rule of association
then there is an opportunity for adaptation. This requires the
designer to: identify a number of plausible rules connecting default
names with their values; and identify evaluation criteria to judge
which rule is appropriate by comparing the behaviour of the rule
against the actual behaviour of the user.

Within the constraints of simple imperative systems the provision
of good defaults is about all we can do to improve the efficiency of the
interface language. Most interfaces make use of a simple notion of
context, but the resources brought to bear on maintaining context are
usually very meagre and the contexts are never such that two
potentially conflicting interpretations might be considered as
alternatives to some piece of user input.

Next we shall consider the potential for adaptation in more
sophisticated systems. A sophisticated system is one which will have
some of the following features on top of a basic imperative language:
facilities to change presentation; facilities to change interaction style;
confirmation language; standard names; and user defined names.

Usually a system incorporating user defined names has the
following components: a syntax for binding names to objects; a syntax
for using defined names; and a syntax for expressing structure in the
environment, e.g. an inheritance hierarchy. The introduction of
structuring in the environment is an attempt to deal with the
problem of "relevance". Structuring deals with the sharing,
commonality and inheritance of properties and the size of name
spaces. However, in dealing with collections of objects, those which

are relevant at any time will be a subset of those which are potentially relevant.

The designer has a choice of strategies to approximate the "actually relevant" objects in any environment. But it is difficult to see how the designer can devise and choose between a suitably parameterised set of strategies such that significant improvements in relevance determination can be achieved. By introducing tense and modality into the language of interaction we have an appropriately richer framework for the discussion of relevance. Some examples of such constructions are:

- modal operators: *always, never, possibly, must, until*

- tense operators: *will, have, had*

The enhanced language of interaction will allow the user to express piecemeal plans; plans which place constraints on the interpretation of future actions, e.g.

I must reply today

I will do that sometime

Possibly before the end of the week

The user is thus able to set up the conditions for the system's interpretation of input. This widens the scope for adaptation considerably because the adaptive system is now able to orient its behaviour to the user's expressed plans. And it leaves the designer of the system with a potentially wide range of strategies for scheduling tasks using: duration, deadline, priority, preference, etc. Evaluation of the strategies is carried out on the basis of comparing the prediction of each strategy with the actual behaviour of the user. Each strategy is an attempt to codify relevance; and the evaluation strategy is an attempt to adjust that codification to the data encountered in use.

Consider a situation in which a group of users take joint responsibility for tasks. Here we might have a constraint which says that if the task involves replying to a letter then it should be replied to within two days. This results in a task of the form:

do TASK before DATE

The designer is faced with two problems: how to deal with an instance of the constraint, and how to distribute the task amongst the community of users. The idea would be to construct a general work distribution strategy and allow the system to adapt this task distribution strategy according to some evaluation criteria. By maintaining performance data on the users' history of success with and acceptance of particular tasks, the system could establish distribution strategies based on user preference, workload, efficiency etc.

In this section we have concentrated on the methods which can be used to enable an adaptive system to successfully interpret its environment; this entails incorporating the notion of context into the system. In particular we have looked at enhancing the language and rules of interaction. For language this includes the use of: demonstratives, names and binding, and tensed sentences. And for rules this includes: default rules, evaluation rules for defaults, relevance determination and evaluation rules for relevance. The use of context in discourse has been exploited in some depth in the implementation of the AID task organiser (Wong and Lesan, 1988). The task organiser is a planning support tool which enables users to plan the production of a multi-author document. Users construct English sentences about tasks and subtasks using dynamic elaborated walk through menus in the spirit of the NaturaLink Interface (Tennant et al., 1983).

The task organiser maintains a context model of the domain of discourse which it uses to keep track of the conversation with the user. Within each context there is knowledge about objects, relations, functions, and relationships with other contexts. From the user's menu selections the organiser builds up a set of constraints on the tasks and sub tasks. For multi-author document preparation these constraints include: the start and end dates of tasks, duration of tasks, allocated responsibility for tasks, availability of personnel, etc.

By keeping track of the changes in particular contexts the interface is able to provide context sensitive responses. The organiser uses the context model to constrain the menu choices available to the user at any one time; regenerating the menus each time a valid utterance is made. The organiser aims to support the user by allowing them to focus on particular contexts whilst keeping them informed of the context sensitive ramifications of their input.

Initially the user is placed into a given context and prompted to reply. The user can then either formulate a reply, ask questions about constraints, or move into another context. The short sample below illustrates the sort of dialogue possible (the selections made from menus by the user are indicated in bold type):

SYSTEM: Do you want to say something about the document preparation task?

USER:

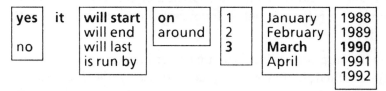

SYSTEM: OK. Anything else, such as its end date, duration or the person in charge of it?

USER:

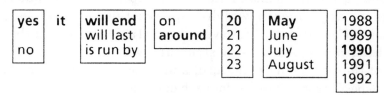

OR

USER:

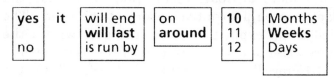

The user's input is put through a simple parser and the resulting user system conversation is echoed in a dialogue window on the screen for the user's convenience. Using the output from the parser the system undertakes:

(i)   Consistency checking. The output is compared against the internal knowledge for a context and any inconsistencies are resolved by a recovery dialogue.

(ii)   Updating. The internal knowledge is updated with the new information.

(iii) Context saturation checking. This evaluates whether everything that needs to be said in a context has been said.

(iv)   Composing a response. The response to the user is determined from the current state of the context.

Whenever a context change occurs, either as a result of a user request or through context saturation, the interaction control cycle for the current context is relinquished in favour of the control cycle for the new context.

The key assumptions behind the task organiser are that although users prefer to schedule the order of a dialogue they also like dialogue which is sensitive to previous interactions. And that by managing context through the use of a context model in conjunction with dynamic walk-through menus it is possible to accommodate both requirements; achieving a more natural discourse. The technique is applicable to any domain which requires the simultaneous management of constraints. However, Grosz (1977) has shown that task oriented dialogues have a structure which parallels the structure of the task being performed, and hence it is necessary to maintain a specific context model for each domain.

User Models

An alternative, but more difficult technique, is to base the mechanism of adaptation on a cognitive theory of the user. The theory is embodied as an explicit model of the user within the interface, and is a representation of some part of the user's mental activity. In the AID project's first exemplar (Totterdell & Cooper 1986), an adaptive user interface front end to the Telecom Gold electronic mail system (Fig. 5.4), much effort was put into implementing a frame-based embedded model of an individual user which sought to map the user's knowledge and experience onto a task model for electronic mail.

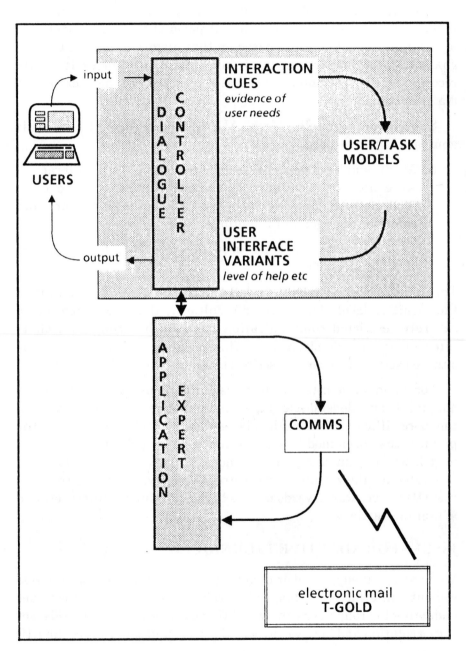

Fig. 5.4 Phase1 architecture for adaptation in a User Interface.

The model recorded the user's history - number of accesses, requests for help, etc. - with different parts of the task model, and used a number of heuristics based on that history to infer the user's goal and their expertise. And from these inferences it would recommend the type and level of dialogue to present the user at each dialogue transaction.

Subsequent exemplars from AID tended to depart from this approach in two respects:

(i) Much simpler models of the history of the user's interaction were used in preference to elaborate models of the user, modelling at the level of a user's behaviour rather than inferring user goals or intentions.

(ii) Distributed models were used in preference to centralised user/task models.

This trend is explained by the relative lack of success in modelling at the cognitive level. One of the difficulties is that the system has a severely restricted communication bandwidth through which to interpret the user's situation. This problem of interpreting the situated action of a user is described eloquently in Suchman (1987).

For an adaptive interface to be useful to its users it must base its adaptation on a dependable model, and the more inferences involved, the more difficult it is to build a dependable model. There is also the problem that user models may be functionally gratuitous; existing models which claim to represent a model of the user have rarely been evaluated for their content or construct validity. Thus the trend on the AID project was towards models based on minimal interpretation of user interactions.

ISSUES FOR ADAPTIVE TECHNIQUES

We have outlined a number of very general techniques for adaptive computer interfaces. In this section we will look at two specific issues - adapting to group needs and weighting evidence. Each of the issues begs a solution and here we present the preferred solutions of the AID project.

Adaptation to a Group of Users - Voting

Sometimes it is necessary for a user interface to adapt to the needs of a group rather than simply adapting to the needs of one individual. In these circumstances it may be necessary to resolve the individual needs as part of a group consensus. We found the metaphor of the democratic vote useful; both for thinking about the problem and as the basis for adaptive mechanisms. The Groupie help interface (Viliunas *et al.* 1988), developed as part of the AID project, incorporated a "first past the post" voting scheme (although earlier designs were based on a form of proportional representation).

The Groupie interface allows experts (also known affectionately as gurus) in a group of users to add their own help to existing system help on a given topic; and individual users are able to choose for themselves the help they prefer or find most helpful. In addition to supporting user-tailorable help, the user interface highlights which guru's help on a topic is preferred by most users. This allows the members of the group, particularly new users, to consult the group's preferred view on a given topic when they don't know whose help to follow.

Adapting the help system's user interface to group needs involves picking up cues from the group members in the form of individual preferences for help and counting these as "votes" for help on a particular topic. The help with the most votes is then "elected" the group-preferred help on that topic and highlighted as such in the help index. Hence,when a guru adds his or her help on a topic this help is put forward as a "candidate" for election as the group-preferred help on that topic.

In the case of Groupie, the voting metaphor was not made explicit to the users because consulting help is a secondary task (and hence of secondary concern) to the user; voting on help was made an implicit part of consulting help. Similarly, contributing help was presented as "changing a help message to what it ought to be" rather than entering an election or a beauty contest. But in other circumstances, giving the voting metaphor a higher user interface profile might well be appropriate, particularly as it is a familiar concept to most users.

The "proportional representation" voting scheme in earlier designs for Groupie ranked all the help on a given topic rather than indicating only the most favoured help. The order in which individual users stacked their "help cards" was taken as their "voting slip". Individual orderings contributed to the group ordering of help for that topic which then influenced (or determined) the order in which help was searched by an individual user, i.e. most favoured help first. This more elaborate voting scheme was found to be unnecessarily complex for a secondary task such as consulting help, and was in danger of becoming intrusive and a distraction from the user's primary task.

Weighting Evidence - The k-Equation

A common problem in modelling an interaction history is the need to give greater weight to evidence, or cues, from recent interactions if circumstances are changing. In some cases, such as the adaptive spelling corrector and adaptive telephone directory, the main objective was to adapt a generic interface to a relatively static individual user need. In other cases, such as the adaptive menu defaults and adaptive task organiser, the main objective was to adapt to, or track, changes of user need. Therefore the relative weight given to recent over past evidence varies.

A solution used in two of the exemplars, the spelling corrector and menu defaults, was to use the following equation to maintain a running average which is weighted towards more recent evidence:

$$\text{new average} = \frac{\text{old average} + (k * \text{new value})}{1 + k}$$

Note that the equation is summing a value, the old average, which represents possibly many previous values with a single new value weighted by k and dividing the result by $1+k$ to keep the new average normalised. That is, the new value is treated as being k times as significant as all previous values put together. For example, a value of $k=1$ treats the new value on its own as being as significant as the sum total of all older values. Therefore, values of $0 < k < 1$ are typical. Note also that setting $k=0$ corresponds to giving no weight to new values and hence can be used to provide a nonadaptive interface.

The k equation is a simple example of a digital filter. It was used to model both relative selection frequencies and relative appropriateness of the three defaulting rules in adaptive menu defaults:

$$\text{new frequency} = \frac{\text{old frequency} + (k * \text{new occurences})}{1 + k}$$

$$\text{new appropriateness} = \frac{\text{old appropriateness} + (k * \text{new evidence})}{1 + k}$$

The same k equation was used to model relative appropriateness of misspelling rules in the adaptive spelling corrector but, in the speller, it was also necessary to accumulate new values (i.e. new evidence) for competing rules over an interval before applying the k equation to determine relative appropriateness. This allowed the k equations for all the rules to keep in step so that they would be comparable for relative appropriateness. For example, for an interval of 18 spelling corrections evidence might be scored and ranked as shown in Fig. 5.5 for missing (M), extra (E), wrong (W) and transposed (T) letters.

```
Misspelling cues                                   New
                                                   evidence

M  M W E M W E M E  E M W M E M M W W

M  M       M      M      M    M   M M            8  M
        E       E    E E        E                5  E
     W       W              W            W W     5  W
                                                 0  T
```

A number of competing (i.e.relative) average values were maintained using the k equation. When new evidence in favour of one (or more) competing value(s) has been collected it is added to the appropriate average value(s) by applying the k equation, and 0 is similarly 'added' to all other competing averages for which no new evidence is found.

This has the effect of "forgetting" accumulated old evidence for averages with no new evidence in step with that of averages with new evidence, i.e. the iteration number, n, is kept in step for all competing averages. If this were not done, the values would not be comparable as they would not all refer equally to the same span of history.

The k equation is an example of a technique for adaptive computer interfaces which requires tuning to the particular situation. Using a two-level adaptor it may be possible to use knowledge of the relationship between task characteristics and k values to automatically tune the weighted average to the demands of the current task. This is an engineering method and is particularly appropriate in situations where formal theory is lacking.

CONCLUSION

In this chapter we have described some of the techniques which have been found useful on the AID project. The techniques were devised as solutions to particular problems and it was only in retrospect that the commonality between these techniques was identified. However it should be added that although it is useful to have a specification of general techniques, much of the interest in the design of adaptive systems comes from designing solutions that satisfy particular contexts. There is neither ready made prescription nor substitute for innovation in the design of adaptive techniques.

This and previous chapters have highlighted the rationale for designing computer adaptive systems and have begun to describe some of the methods which are available to support the construction of these systems. The aim is to produce systems which are better fitted to their users. It is assumed that this fit will reveal itself in performance indicators of the user such as increased throughput, rate of learning, improved understanding, or greater accuracy etc. However, we need to evaluate these indicators in order to test the fit. In the next chapter we look at evaluation methods in more detail.

Chapter 6
The Evaluation of Adaptive Systems

P. Totterdell and E. Boyle

Central to progress in the design and validation of computer adaptive systems will be possession of the means to evaluate the performance of this type of system. In addition to procedures for measuring the total performance of the system - its ability to adapt and to affect behavioral measures - we also require evaluation procedures that support the design process. These latter procedures will support the diagnosis of the relationship between the design and its performance in order to improve subsequent design. It is also expected that some of these evaluation techniques will be embodied within the system to allow it to self regulate its performance.

In this chapter we first examine different types of evaluation for human computer interaction. Then we look at some of the special problems of evaluating adaptive systems. Following this, a number of different techniques for evaluation which have been developed and used on the AID project are described. And finally we examine the application of these techniques during and after the design and construction of a computer adaptive system (cf. Boyle, 1988).

FORMATIVE AND SUMMATIVE EVALUATION

Evaluation of interfaces often occurs (where it occurs at all) after the interface has been built. But evaluation of a system at an earlier stage in development can highlight basic flaws in the design of the system which might not otherwise become evident until a later stage; at which point modification of the system would probably be much more complicated and time consuming.

It was in the context of educational and social action programs that Scriven (1972) first discussed the importance of both formative evaluation, which is evaluation during the development of a system, and summative evaluation which is evaluation of the final system. As applied to the development of computer systems, formative evaluation involves monitoring the system during its development with a view to identifying any modifications or improvements which can be made in future system development. Summative evaluation involves an assessment of the overall performance of the system in terms of the impact, usability and effectiveness of the system.

Formative evaluation puts the emphasis on open-ended techniques for gathering information such as interviews, questionnaires, attitude surveys and scaling techniques whilst summative evaluation commonly focuses on a more restricted quantitative assessment of the system's impact and effectiveness using such measures as response time and error rate. However, both qualitative and quantitative techniques may be appropriate at either stage in system development.

Howard and Murray (1987) distinguish between comparative and diagnostic evaluation. Comparative evaluation is used to compare the performance of a system against another system whilst diagnostic evaluation assesses the performance of a system with respect to certain absolute criteria of usability.

It is felt by some researchers working in the area of the development of human-computer interfaces that comparative evaluation has been used where it is not strictly appropriate. Computers often offer new ways of doing things and it is therefore not always possible to compare performance with an existing system lacking the added functionality of the new system. Similarly the results from a comparative study are often not instructive for design;

they merely indicate that one system outperforms another within a very restricted set of circumstances. In the area of human computer interaction, the overuse of comparative evaluation has been criticised because the interface frequently involves many different variables and it is not always possible to conclude that an observed effect can be unambiguously attributed to the variable under investigation (Brooks & Alty, 1985).

A further distinction is drawn by Howard and Murray (1987) between explicit and implicit evaluation. Implicit evaluation is an informal subjective evaluation of the interface, usually by the designer, during its design and includes hunches, design experience and analogical knowledge of previous systems. Explicit evaluation is a more formal experimental approach to evaluation and involves identifying evaluation objectives and then planning and undertaking experiments which establish those objectives.

The different types of evaluation described should also fit a process of iterative design and evaluation which has been shown to be an effective way of developing human-computer interfaces (Gould et al., 1987; Hewett, 1986). In this process the design is modified in a number of cycles of design, test and redesign. Each cycle involves a number of stages and at each stage in the cycle there is an opportunity for evaluation. As with formative and summative evaluation different evaluation techniques will be appropriate at different stages.

Several useful papers on how to conduct an evaluation of a human- computer interface have been published. Malone et al. (1984) detailed ten specific steps which should be carried out in evaluating a human-computer interface. Howard and Murray (1987) have classified the different techniques used in evaluation and have proposed an "evaluation plan" which described the steps in carrying out an evaluation. They also proposed an "evaluation environment" detailing the variables which need to be considered in identifying the appropriate techniques to use in evaluation.

Essential steps for evaluation include:

- Identifying the purposes or objectives of the evaluation. This includes identifying: the commissioner of the study, the audience and most importantly the criteria or reasons for the study.

- Experimental design. This includes prior identification of suitable methods, subjects, tasks, measurements, experimental setting, and resources.

- Collecting the results. This involves running the experiments and collecting relevant data.

- Analysing data. This involves using suitable analysis frameworks or statistical techniques or both.

- Drawing conclusions. This involves either making recommendations for modifications to the system or making generalised observations and further proposals for evaluation or concluding that everything is satisfactory.

The evaluation of an adaptive system will also follow these same steps but there a number of specific problems in finding suitable methods for evaluation because of the nature of adaptive processes. These problems will be outlined in the next section.

PROBLEMS IN EVALUATING ADAPTIVE SYSTEMS

To carry out a comparative evaluation of an adaptive system it is necessary to identify an appropriate system against which to compare performance. This will usually be a non-adaptive system which is sometimes referred to as a static system. If adaptation is taking place along a number of dimensions it will be necessary to provide a non-adaptive or static comparison for each dimension.

Non-adaptive Controls

The adaptive system's behavior can range over a set of possible states for any given dimension of adaptation. The question, therefore, is which of these states should the evaluator choose for the non-adaptive control. Where appropriate the state might be selected by best current practice. For example Greenberg and Witten (1985) constructed an adaptive system for a telephone directory access task which altered the ordering of options on the menus in response to individual usage data as a means of increasing retrieval speed. To form the control they defined a plausible static interface presentation which divided the ranges of names equally over the menus.

Greenberg and Witten - Adaptive telephone directory system

> Greenberg & Witten (1985) made a limited study of telephone usage patterns and found that in normal usage almost 60% of the numbers called had been dialled previously. The pattern of usage approximated a Zipf distribution. Thus given the history of an individual's past usage it would be possible to estimate the probability of each number being called again. Greenberg and Witten built and evaluated two systems which allowed access to a directory of telephone numbers via a hierarchy of menus.
>
> In the first system, the static system, the directory entries comprising the database were divided into subranges which covered equal portions of the alphabet. Users selected from menus the subrange option containing the desired name until a menu was reached which contained that name as an option. Hence, to retrieve any name from the directory required the user to descend through a constant number of menus.
>
> The second system, the adaptive system, presented directory entries at a level in the hierarchy corresponding to their likelihood of being selected. With the history of an individual's previous calls and an approximation to the Zipf distribution it is possible to estimate the probability of selection of each entry in the directory and to split the subranges so that the most frequently used names will appear higher in the menu tree. The menu tree was arranged so that each menu option had an approximately equal probability of being selected. The intention was to reduce the mean number of key presses required to retrieve an item. Greenberg and Witten hypothesised that reducing the mean search depth would result in reduced mean time per selection.

However, there may not always be a plausible control; particularly if the system is a novel application for which there is no existing counterpart. One option would be to sample randomly from the set of states over which the behaviour of the adaptive system ranges and to use the randomly chosen states as the static control. The states cannot, however, be sampled dynamically during a trial session because of the possible affect on user performance of presenting an inconsistent interface; this would effectively prevent the user from forming a predictive model of the interface.

Using a between-subjects design, in which each treatment contains one system state sampled from the range of possible states, may not be an ideal comparison either. Instead, if there is a best state - or set of equivalent best states - which facilitate performance for a wide range of potential users then one of these states should be the static control. This is because an adaptive system will perform sub-optimally during a discovery process, and therefore if there is only a single best state then usually it would have been better to determine that state experimentally than to have an adaptive system discover the state, i.e. the inefficiency of finding the state should, where it confers no other advantage, be kept outside of the run-time system. However, the inefficiency of discovery is justified in situations where there are a set of incompatible states which if accommodated by using an adaptive mechanism will give a performance function which is better than the performance function of a system using a single best state. And for this reason one should use the single best state as the control and evaluate whether the adaptive system can utilise incompatible states to outperform the control. A set of incompatible states is a good indicator of variability in the environment.

Unfortunately, the recommendation to use the best state as the static control is complicated by the fact that in all but the simplest situations there will be a very large space of potential states; and the designer and evaluator may be unaware of some of these states. For example, in the case of the telephone directory we might consider all permutations of alphabetical ordering but there are a multitude of other presentation formats such as numerical ordering, organisational ordering etc., all of which might contain the best single state. So we are forced to strictly define the set of states over which our evaluation assessment holds true.

Another problem with the use of a non-adaptive control is that we are forced to define the adaptive system's performance with respect to one or more points of equilibrium - that is we must say when the system has adapted and use that as the state to be compared with the non-adaptive control. However, adaptation is a dynamic process in which both partners in the interaction can be in a state of flux because of either their mutual affects or through external constraints; and we must therefore rely more often on categorical assessments of steady states of the system rather than on discrete points of equilibrium. This forces us to choose the intervals over which measurements will be taken of the adaptive system. This can be problematic. For example, an adaptive system may take some time to gather information about its environment - should this initial period of inefficiency be included within the interval for comparison?

Greenberg and Witten (1985), for example, chose to ignore this acquisition period by priming their adaptive system with usage data; data which in normal circumstances the system would have had to accumulate over a period of time. Robertson *et al.* (1987) were unsatisfied by this choice of control because it both gives the adaptive system an unrealistic advantage, and it ignores the possible learning effects that might take place in a real scenario where the user has to learn on a system which is at first unadapted but then becomes adapted. The other concern was that in a real setting the usage of the system was likely to be sporadic whereas Greenberg and Witten (1985) chose a continuous selection task for their evaluation.

In some applications the period or periods of inefficiency will be small in comparison to the lifecycle. In the telephone directory retrieval task it is clear that for users who repeatedly access the same numbers over a long time period, the problems of the acquisition period may not be a cause for concern because of the potential overriding benefits over the complete usage period. It is clear, therefore, that the evaluator must give due regard to the probable context of use in choosing their comparisons. The evaluator may also take as part of their remit the task of describing at what point the adaptive system becomes effective in comparison to the non-adaptive control.

The problem of intervals for comparison can apply equally to choosing the termination point for the evaluation as well as to its commencement. For example let us take the case of the adaptive spelling corrector, which adapts according to the frequency of errors made by a user and orders the displayed list of possible corrections accordingly so that the most likely one will be at the top of the list. On this basis it will reduce selection time. Over time, it is reasonable to suggest that the user would learn not to make those errors. The user's pattern of errors would therefore change and the total number of errors made by the user would decrease. Theoretically at least the adaptation would eventually become redundant as the user would make no errors. And theoretically our non-adaptive control, which also highlights corrections but in no particular order, would also eliminate errors. As the number of errors tends to zero the reduction in selection time gained from ordering the corrections will also tend to zero. So the evaluator should be aware that there may be a point at which the adaptation stops being effective.

In this example, the adaptation ceased being effective because the conditions for its effectiveness had been removed. We could of course have made the example even more surprising by making the very purpose of the adaptation the requirement to eliminate its own conditions for being. Thus, if we had a theory that said we could eliminate errors more quickly by presenting high frequency errors on their own rather than presenting all frequencies of errors together, then the adaptive systems purpose would be to eliminate errors as quickly as possible and hence to make itself redundant!

Dynamics of Adaptive Behaviour

So far our discussion of evaluation has centred on the problem of illustrating that the adaptive system converges on a state which gives it a performance advantage over a non-adaptive counterpart. We have already hinted, however, that there may be a stronger requirement on an adaptive system - that it can adapt to at least two mutually incompatible criteria. This is in fact the same definition that Martens (1959) proposes as a test for machine learning. A system with a fixed control strategy will not satisfy this definition, hence opening the way for a special class of behaviour - adaptive dynamics (Gaines, 1972) - and associated mechanisms requiring explanation.

If we accept this stronger requirement then the burden of the evaluator is to show not only that the system is able to facilitate performance but also that there are different "optima" in the environment and that the system can find these "optima". That is, enhanced performance must be explainable in terms of the use of information about a particular user, group, task, etc., which if applied to another user, group or task would result in depressed performance by comparison. In the next section we describe an experimental method which will test whether a system meets these criteria.

However, even with this additional requirement the focus is still on the terminal states of adaptation and not on the process of change between states. But as Gaines (1972) observes, adaptation in a system is not instantaneous; it is "... a function not only of the immediate environment but also of its previous states ... it is this sequential dependence, or memory, inherent in the behaviour of most adaptive systems, which gives rise to most of the complexity of adaptive behaviour". An adaptive system "becomes satisfactory through its experience of the environment, and may possibly become unsatisfactory again" (Gaines, 1972).

Gaines therefore bases his definitions of different modes of adaptive behaviour on the concept of a task as a segment of interaction which can be said to be either satisfactory or unsatisfactory. And for the purpose of evaluating the adaptive dynamics of a system we are particularly interested in repeated task sequences because, as Gaines points out, these allow us to characterise the adaptive system's ability to change response to the same situation.

Paraphrasing, the three modes of adaptive behaviour are: potentially adaptive in which the system is potentially adaptive to a set of tasks but having adapted to one task it may no longer be potentially adaptive to the others; compatibly adaptive in which the system having adapted to one task remains potentially adaptive to the others; and jointly adaptive in which the system having adapted to one task has also become adapted to the others.

The compatibly adaptive system is the one which we are looking for in Marten's incompatible criteria test. But to ensure that the system is not simply a static controller which has a strategy suited to two situations we must add to our evaluation the condition suggested by Gaines (1972) that the interaction be acceptable but not immediately acceptable. That is we look for adaptive dynamics.

Beyond this we could begin to add even stricter criteria on what will and won't pass as an adaptive system. For example, we might require that the system performs satisfactorily within a reasonable time period (Wilkinson, 1987). However, such considerations will

largely be pragmatic; for example in the context of genetics we may
be talking about very long time periods indeed.

Self-evaluation

One of the features of complex adaptive systems that was introduced
in Chapter 3 was the ability of the system to monitor and evaluate the
success of its own behaviour. In the first instance this will manifest
itself in the form of a simple feedback loop but as the system gains in
complexity we are forced to introduce meta-level considerations such
as the capability of the system to pre-evaluate a course of action and
even to evaluate its own evaluation function.

The interesting aspect of this from an evaluation point of view is
that we are expecting the system to run its own experiments! And to
achieve this end we will need to encode evaluation expertise within
the system. The problem, however, is that the system has only a very
limited access to contextual information. For example, it is not too
difficult to produce a system which can monitor and use error rates to
change its behaviour but it is more difficult to enable the system to
evaluate the relationship between error rate and user satisfaction. It
is likely, therefore, that for the foreseeable future the evaluator's role
will continue to be to run formative and summative evaluations
which investigate the wider considerations of adaptive systems such
as their social context; and that they will also be involved in
producing specifications of experimental designs to be encoded as part
of the system's architecture.

The argument presented here parallels that of the deferred design
method discussed earlier. That is we are seeing the beginnings of a
trend to delegate functions to the system which are normally retained
outside the system as part of the wider social system. No
functionality is being added to the total (social) system, it is simply
being moved to a different part of the total system. Deferred design
recognises that we cannot fix all parameters in advance; and self
evaluation recognises that the system requires a basis on which to fix
the parameters.

A system which is able to assess its own performance and change
its behaviour accordingly has been termed a self-regulating system
(Trevellyan and Browne, 1987). Trevellyan and Browne built a self
regulating version of the telephone number retrieval system

developed by Greenberg and Witten (1985). Two strategies were embodied in the self-regulating system: to adapt the content of the menus on the basis of user access to data items, à la Greenberg and Witten; and to use a fall back strategy of providing a static system when performance with the previous strategy falls below a baseline measure. In order to make a system self-regulating in this way the system must have: some means of measuring performance along the relevant dimension; a target level of performance; some means of assessing whether this target performance has been achieved; and the capacity to alter the system's response on the basis of the results.

From an evaluation perspective the difficulty of providing systems with a baseline measure looks considerable. One method would be to run experiments on a static system to produce standard response times or error rates for given conditions. In some instances it will be possible for the system to dynamically build a model of how the system would be performing if the alternative strategy or strategies were being used. In the telephone number retrieval task, the system actually uses the first hundred calls to find the mean search depth for a static system. If there is little difference between the mean depth for the static strategy and that for the usage strategy, the advantages of the consistency of the static strategy will probably outweigh the advantages of the usage strategy. The usage strategy best meets the system's objectives when user interaction describes a Zipf distribution but not when it describes a flat distribution where all items are equally likely to be accessed.

In the self-regulating system we have described there was no facility for turning the usage strategy back on once it had gone out of favour. This would have been relatively easy to provide, simply by monitoring the user model for a change in the distribution of calls and turning the strategy back on if the distribution starts to approximate a Zipf distribution. However, this will not guarantee that time per selection is reduced. The problem of managing the application of strategies will increase as we introduce more strategies because of the potential interaction between strategies and the changes occurring within the user over time. This problem is discussed more fully in the section on stability and change.

TECHNIQUES FOR EVALUATING ADAPTIVE SYSTEMS

Our intention in this section is to describe a few of the techniques for evaluating adaptive systems which have been used and found useful on the AID project.

Metrics

The project developed a set of metrics to represent the categories of data essential to adaptive systems. These metrics, which were described in Chapter 2, have been found useful in the evaluation of adaptive systems. Fig. 6.1 shows the role of the metrics in evaluation by relating each of the metrics to the components of a logical system. The trigger metric (Trig. M.) and theory assessment metric (Tass. M.) are both captured by the monitor and conveyed to the user model or theory based part of the system. The recommendation metric (Rec. M.) characterises the recommendations for interface changes given by the theory. The implementation metric (Imp. M.) refers to the general functioning of the system. The objective metric (Obj. M.) will need to be captured by the evaluator if it cannot be captured directly by the system. And finally the generality metric (Gen. M.) will be assessed by the evaluator through their characterisation of the user and application domain.

Here are an example set of metrics for the self regulating system of Trevellyan & Browne (1987) :

Objective metric. - Given that the objective of providing the adaptive interface was one of allowing users to make selections more quickly, the objective metric was time based. This objective metric could be measured on-line so the monitor embedded in the system was designed and built to automatically capture the time taken to make a selection.

Theory assessment metric - The theory embedded in the system simply posits that offering the frequently selected items at a high level in the menu hierarchy will reduce the time spent accessing selections. Although presenting items at a higher level in the menu hierarchy will reduce the number of menus traversed this does not necessarily imply that time per selection will be reduced. To verify

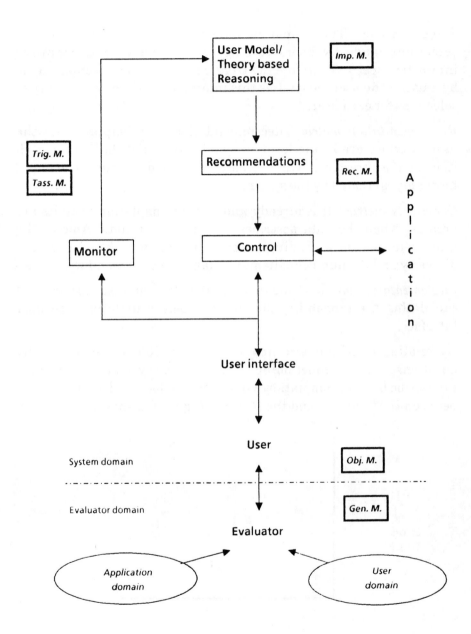

Fig. 6.1 Role of metrics in evaluating adaptive systems.

this theory the number of keystrokes per selection was recorded as well as the time per selection recorded in the objective metric.

Trigger metric - The system assumes that knowing the successful selections made by users can be used effectively to improve interaction speed. Therefore the trigger metric is the selections made by a user. The user model uses this information to create a history of selections for each user.

Recommendation metric - Recommendations for adaptation of the user interface are in the form of a probability distribution for each item in the directory. On the basis of this distribution a menu hierarchy is created by the system.

Generality metric - It is already known that adaptation benefits are greatest when the data describes a Zipf distribution. Among the unknowns for these findings are the effect that the size of the directory and the number of items displayed on each menu will have.

Implementation metric - This includes the effect on response delay of calculating the probability distribution before updating the user interface.

By relating metrics one to another it is possible to answer many questions about the functioning of the adaptive system. For example to describe how the adaptation will behave we look at the relationship between the Trig. M. and the Rec. M. Figure 6.2 shows a case for a

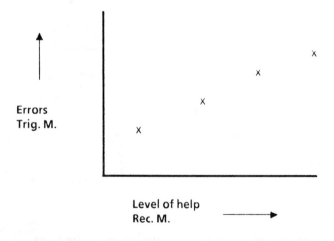

Fig. 6.2 System behaviour.

different adaptive system where number of errors are used as the basis for recommending help. The graph illustrates that the system provides more help as the user makes more errors.

The system's theory is that by adjusting the level of help it can increase the speed of interaction (Tass. M.) and hence increase user satisfaction (Obj. M.). To assess the impact of the adaptive changes on the user's interaction with the system, we need to look at the relationship between Tass. M. and Rec. M. Fig. 6.3 shows that the

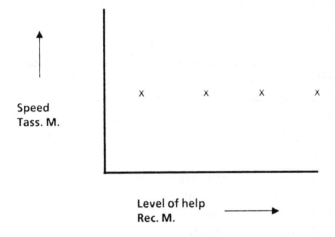

Fig. 6.3 Effect of theory on interaction.

theory's recommendations for changing level of help is having no impact on the speed of interaction - hence the theory is ineffective. If the relationship hoped for was found the evaluator would still need to look at the relationship between Tass. M. and Obj. M. in order to determine whether the adaptive system is succeeding in meeting its objective because of the theory.

Niche Description

The niche description is a technique for early evaluation developed on the AID project (Totterdell *et al.*, 1989) which enables a designer to describe the implications of their design proposal with respect to both the projected benefits conferred on the user and the goodness of fit with user characteristics. The technique is viewed as an alternative to design analysis methods which rely on decompositional mappings between the user's world and the system model, e.g. PAD (Keane & Johnson, 1987).

In Chapter 3 we made the point that adaptive systems are only adaptive in the context of a particular environment and that to refer to something as adaptive we must have knowledge of the external referents of its behaviour. Here we can make use of the concept of a notional world (Dennett, 1978); which for an adaptive system is the world or environment in which the system would be perfectly adapted. Bechtel (1985) describes the notional world as:

> "a fictional world that would be a perfect niche for a system with a particular set of internal states (i.e. a world in which the system would be perfectly adapted). The notional world of a system will usually partly correspond to the world the system actually inhabits ... but it may differ in some respects ... what we are doing is tantamount to saying that the internal states of the system make it best adapted to a world which differs in various ways from the one it inhabits."

The notional world applies equally to non-adaptive systems, the non-adaptive system simply puts tighter bounds on its notional world by assuming that the world does not differ along the dimensions indicated by an adaptive counterpart.

The niche description is a technique for describing the notional world of a system and is used to determine what a design is good for and where it will fit. To construct the niche description the designer or evaluator teases out the implicit assumptions about the world held within a design, so that the assumptions can be informally or empirically validated.

The assumptions in the niche description can be split into two categories: transforming assumptions which say something about the added value of a design; and operational assumptions which say something about how the world must be for the system to work. Fig. 6.4 subdivides these categories further.

We can compare these categories with the metrics already described. The transformational categories are similar to the objective metric. The difference is that the objective metric focuses on the purpose of adaptation in a system whereas the transformational assumptions are intended to provide a much broader description of

Assumptions	Examples
Transforming assumptions	
Benefits to the user	User feels more in control
Non-disruptive change	Additional dialogue will not frustrate user
Operational assumptions	
User characteristics	User reads from left to right
Adequacy of model	Patterns of use are detectable by the system

Fig. 6.4 Categories of assumption for a niche description.

the social effects of a system. We can also compare the theory assessment metric to the user characteristics category. The theory assessment metric describes those parts of the system which rely on the existence of particular environmental characteristics in order for the adaptation to work. The user characteristics category is a broader description of all the assumed characteristics of the user which are sources for the system as a whole. The trigger metric, recommendation metric and implementation metric provide a detailed breakdown of the adequacy of model category. And finally the whole of the niche description serves the role of the generality metric in that it specifies the conditions which must prevail in the environment for the design to be successful.

The use of the niche description was applied to the evaluation of adaptive menu defaults described in the previous chapter. Essentially, the adaptive defaulter worked by recognising and using patterns of selections in a user's menu usage to predict the user's next menu selection. If the user history indicates that the user is performing a number of "cut" and "paste" operations then the adaptive defaulter will offer "paste" as the default selection following a "cut" operation.

The assumptions underlying the adaptive defaulter (Rautenbach, 1988) were:

User benefit. - "Users like menus to offer a default selection as long as this selection is usually the one they were going to select". A small observational survey showed this assumption to be untrue because users often pop up a menu for purposes of browsing and don't expect to invoke an operation if they then release the mouse button. To remedy this problem the cursor was placed next to the predicted option rather than on it so that releasing the mouse button caused a null operation.

Non disruptive change. - "Dynamically changing the basis on which defaults are chosen will not confuse the user". Subsequent observation showed that the changes were in fact unobtrusive; and that some users were unable to say what had changed. So this assumption was warranted.

User characteristics. - "Menu use exhibits characteristic patterns of selections which require different defaulting rules". The system was built so that it could log the sequence of selections from each menu. These selection histories were used as part of an off-line analysis to evaluate whether the patterns predicted do occur in actual use. The selection logs for two users were collected over a period of two weeks. The results indicated that the patterns do exist. However, the data also showed that of the 156 instances of menus which had been used only nineteen had logs of more than twenty selections which implies that many menus are used infrequently.

Adequacy of model. - "The patterns of use persist long enough to adapt defaults to them". The evaluation showed that the three pattern detection rules often overlapped in their prediction of the next selection. This might suggest that there is little advantage to having three rules instead of one. However, for the nineteen menus with logs of more than twenty selections, the adaptive system which swapped between the three rules did show a performance advantage over each of the rules taken separately. The adaptive system predicted correctly for 56% of selections, whilst the three rules predicted correctly for 49%, 52% and 51% of selections. However, an analysis of variance (Leiser *et al.*, 1988) showed that this difference was not significant.

If the evaluation shows that an adaptive system can be supported in its assumptions then it still remains to evaluate whether the adaptive system fulfills its overall objective, which in the case of adaptive menu defaults is to quicken usage of the system. To evaluate this for the adaptive menu defaults it will be necessary to collect comparative measures of the time taken to complete a number of tasks over an extended period with the adaptive and non-adaptive systems.

Identifying the assumptions which underlie a design, whether it be in the form described or otherwise, has been found useful for both identifying those designs which rest on 'shaky ground' and for determining the evaluation experiments which need to be undertaken to confirm or reject whether the assumptions hold for the intended context of use.

A Diagnostic Technique

In our description of the metrics of adaptive system design we discussed the importance of being able to relate the changes that the adaptive system makes at the interface (Rec. M.) to both the theory (Tass. M.) and triggers (Trig. M.) on which the changes are made. In this section we describe a study which explicitly addressed this problem in order to evaluate the user model of an adaptive system.

The first adaptive system which the AID project built was an interface to an existing electronic mail system. The system is described in Totterdell & Cooper (1986), and its evaluation in Hockley (1986).

The user model in the system mapped a user's actions against a set of simple linear plans which described the possible sets of commands that users could execute to achieve application tasks. An individual history of the user's experience and difficulties with commands and tasks was maintained as part of an explicit user model within the interface. As well as tracking the user's context, the user model was used to infer the user's level of skill with particular tasks and recommended the level of guidance to be used in the dialogue with the user.

Functionality was included in the design of the system so that it could be used in an experimental context. The system allowed the evaluator to monitor activity in various modules of the system such as the user model. Various parameters of the system could be changed between sessions for the purposes of evaluation. For example, individual dimensions of adaptation such as the level of guidance could be enabled or disabled to allow for comparative evaluation.

Nine subjects of mixed computer experience were used in the evaluation study. Six subjects were used in the adaptive condition with all dimensions of adaptation turned on and three in the non-adaptive condition with the dimensions disabled. Each subject used the system for three half hour sessions separated by three days. Their task was to respond to nine letters in their electronic mail in-tray. A video recording of the screen was made and system logs collected. Also subjects provided a concurrent and a retrospective verbal protocol of their behaviour.

The evaluation of the interface included an assessment of the success of the user model. Two types of assessment were made of the user model: an assessment of the accuracy of the model's inferences about user difficulties; and an assessment of the effectiveness of the changes made at the interface.

The user model's inferences were judged by comparing the model's detection of user difficulties against the user's own statements of their difficulties. The measures were the percentage of user difficulties correctly inferred by the model and the percentage of false positive inferences of difficulties. A random sample of 180 user commands showed that the model detected 40% of the difficulties referred to by the subjects but at the expense of a false positive rate of 53%.

The user model embodies a crude theory of human performance which predicts that experienced users require little guidance and are hindered by too much, while inexperienced users require more guidance. The level of guidance is predicted on the strength of a weighted average of errors and requests for help on specific commands by individual users. To assess the utility of the changes made to the level of guidance an independent expert was asked to rate each change as to whether or not it was in the right direction and useful depending on the user's declared or apparent difficulties. Of the sixty eight changes in level of guidance resulting from the 180 user commands those judged useful were: 18% of the changes based on inferred difficulties, none of the changes based on inferred expertise, and overall only 7% of the changes.

The comparative performance of the adaptive interface against the non-adaptive interface was measured by the subject's command entry rate, task completion rate and goal achievement rate. Deleting a message would be an example of a task, and the complete processing of a message would be an example of a goal. These measures showed a small but general performance advantage for the non-adaptive system. The user modelling diagnostics, however, suggest that one reason for the poor performance of the adaptive system was that although it was able to detect 40% of user difficulties, only in 7% of the cases was it able to put the information to good use. And this indicates that the theory embodied in the system should be revised. It should also be noted, however, that overall performance was low in both conditions. This was attributed to the poor quality of the screen design and may have affected the comparison.

Subjects' opinions were also canvassed using two questionnaires. The first asked the subjects their opinion of ease of use factors. The second required them to select the statements they agreed with from a range of positive and negative statements about the interface. Difference of opinions between the adaptive and non-adaptive conditions were negligible.

From the information collected in the evaluation it was possible to make a number of recommendations for improving the design of the adaptive interface. It was suggested that the user model could make better use of the data by propagating inferences rather than treating different parts of the task network as independent. For example, expertise in one part of the network may suggest competence in another part. The user model also incorrectly assumed that usage of a command is an indicator of expertise whereas in fact it may be an indicator that the user is experimenting. More importantly the inferences made in the user model could have been put to better use by linking them to qualitative rather than quantitative changes in guidance.

The significance of the study to the evaluation of adaptive systems was that it demonstrated the importance of being able to measure the behaviour of different parts of the system in order to understand the performance of the system as a whole.

TESTING FOR ADAPTATION

The experimental paradigm that is usually adopted to evaluate adaptive systems is the comparison between the adaptive and non-adaptive system. Any performance difference that results between the two conditions is assumed to be attributable to adaptation because there is no difference between the two systems apart from the added functionality which the designers have labelled adaptive. But this does not tell us whether that functionality is in fact adaptive. And we need some criteria and an experimental design which will allow us to evaluate the designer's claim.

A weak criterion for an adaptive system is that it is a system which changes its behaviour in response to inputs such that it is better suited to its task. However, as we saw in the previous section a stronger criterion is that the system should be able to change its response to inputs from at least two mutually incompatible sources such that it becomes suited to the current task but remains able to adapt to the other sources. For human-computer interaction, we are talking about a system that can act on a perceived difference between users, groups of users, or tasks, to change its behaviour such that the change correlates with the perceived difference and brings about improved performance with respect to a given purpose or purposes.

Take the case of two user populations, U1 and U2, which differ along some dimension or dimensions. If the adaptive system, S, can detect this difference and can organise its behaviour to take account of the difference so as to facilitate a performance measure, then allowing the two user populations to interact with S will result in the system reaching different states, S1 and S2, for the two populations. This is the first of the two conditions depicted in Fig. 6.5. X is an

Condition		Performance
1. Adapted	U1 - S1 U2 - S2	X
2. Mal-adapted	U1 - S2 U2 - S1	Y

Fig. 6.5 Experimental design to test for adaptive behaviour.

overall measure of performance in this condition. In the second condition, the system states have been swapped such that U1 receives S2, and U2 receives S1, that is the users interact with a system which is adapted to another population but which is maladapted to themselves; Y is an overall measure of performance in this condition.

If the designers have been correct in their assumptions then we would expect performance Y to be inferior to performance X.

However, if there is no statistical difference between X and Y then we cannot say whether it was because there was no difference in the user populations on the chosen dimension or whether it was because the system could not organise its behaviour to account for the difference.

The test is designed to determine whether the system can organise its behaviour for one user population in a fashion which is presently unsuited to another user population but to whom it can adapt given time. The situation is illustrated in Fig. 6.6.

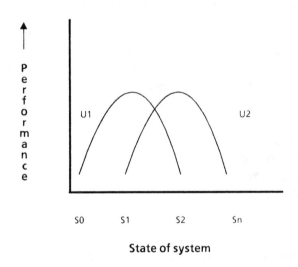

Fig. 6.6 Graphical representation of test for adaptive behaviour.

Assuming that there is a difference between the two populations, then we know that there is a system state where:

Performance(S1, U1) > Performance(S1, U2)

We must also show that the system can find another state where:

Performance(S2, U2) > Performance(S2, U1)

Unfortunately the test hides a number of problems. The experimental design will have to control for order effects. Users cannot all be given the adapted condition first and then the maladapted condition or vice versa because of the possible transfer effects between conditions. A good example of the problem is that the system might be employing a fixed control strategy, c, which brings the system into an adapted state for U1 and which if then applied again with U2 also brings the system into an adapted state. We can eliminate this chance effect by also applying c to U2 before U1.

The obvious solution to the ordering problem would be to give half the users the maladapted condition first. However, the maladapted condition is normally derived from an adapted condition. This is part of the strength of the test because it means we do not have to specify the population difference in advance and similarly we do not have to specify the system states that will constitute the adapted and maladapted states in advance of running the experiment.

One solution is to give users a pretest learning phase to allow the evaluator to establish the adapted and maladapted states. The advantage is that the dynamics of adaptation will be buried within the learning phase so that the evaluator can establish two fixed states for the test - remember that as soon as the user receives a maladapted system it will begin to adapt to them. Of course, this simply shifts the ordering problem into the learning phase but as long as we ensure that subjects receive both conditions for an equivalent amount of time and that an equal number receive each condition immediately prior to the test phase (which is possible by sequencing users) then a balanced design is achievable.

The test for adaptiveness was applied as part of the evaluation of the Groupie interface. The interface was described in more detail in previous chapters but essentially it is an adaptive interface developed on the AID project which provides members of a group with the facility to produce help messages for use by others within the group. In the earlier version of the interface the messages were rated by members of the group and the ratings determined the retrieval order for the messages. Hence different groups could produce different help messages and different retrieval orders.

Here we summarise the evaluation of the adaptiveness of the first version of Groupie (Viliunas, Wong and Totterdell, 1988). A set of help messages giving alternative interpretations of the fields of a form were rated by two groups of users each of which was given an alternative scenario for the form. This resulted in two versions of the system S1 and S2. Two groups of five users were then given either S1 or S2 and both were given two form-filling tasks. The tasks were suited to either the scenario which resulted in S1 or the scenario which resulted in S2. Hence for each subject, the system they used was adapted to one of the tasks and maladapted to the other. The order of presentation of the two tasks was balanced to eliminate order effects.

The null hypothesis was that a group of users using an adapted version of Groupie would not differ significantly in the accuracy with which they completed a form filling task from a group of users using a non-adapted version. A Wilcoxon test showed there to be a significant difference ($Z = 2.803$, $N = 10$, two tailed, $p < 0.05$) between the adapted and non-adapted conditions.

The results indicated that: the content of the help messages was of sufficient quality to show a performance effect, there were differences in the help requirements of groups undertaking different task scenarios, and that Groupie was able to reconfigure its help messages to reflect those different requirements.

STABILITY AND CHANGE

One of the most difficult problems in designing adaptive systems is formulating the policy or the tactics for change which will be embodied in the control strategy of the system. The difficulty arises because of the reciprocal relationship between the system and its interactive environment. In the case where the interactive environment consists of end users, the designer must be aware that the users which they are trying to bring under the "control" of the system's behavioural repertoire are dynamic. The users will not only be able to vary their response because of their interactions outside the interactive partnership but may also modify their responses because of the effect of the partnership.

This may confound the system in its attempt to attribute change to specific system factors. For example, a system which attempts to reduce user anxiety levels by adjusting its explanation types might succeed because the user is pleased by its very attempt at accommodation rather than because of the transfigured explanation. Likewise a teaching system which infers user expertise in order to effectively enhance user comprehension must be prepared to modify its inferences because of the effect it has on the learner.

A confounding factor in this problem is that change itself plays a part in the behaviour of the partnership. A system which rapidly switches between strategies may be very disruptive from the user's viewpoint, and the system must determine whether performance is debilitated because of the failure of the strategy (tempting another change), or because of the change itself. Hence, an understanding of the tradeoff between stability and change will be an important determinant of the efficiency with which we can design and build adaptive systems. And we must attempt to endow computer adaptive systems with the property of timeliness for the management of change.

A series of empirical studies were initiated on the AID project to investigate aspects of this problem. The stages are reported here as an example of the contribution that empirical investigation can make to support the design of adaptive systems. The studies were prompted by Greenberg & Witten's (1985) work, described earlier.

They tested the adaptive system against the static system using data from an individual's telephone usage. The adaptive system was primed using the first 122 of these calls and subjects were required to make a further thirty eight selections; the first eight of these were for practice. The results were:

- a reduction of 32% in mean search depth from the static to the adaptive system;

- a reduction of 35% in time per selection from the static to the adaptive system;

- no difference in time per menu between the two systems;

- a 40% reduction in errors per menu from the static to the adaptive system;

- a 60% reduction in errors per selection from the static to the adaptive system.

It was also stated that most subjects preferred the adaptive system because of "... the apparently shorter paths for repetitive names ... ".

Trevellyan and Browne (1987) carried out a replication and extension of Greenberg and Witten's work. They conjectured that had the original experiment consisted of a larger number of trials then it might be expected that subjects using the static system would have become familiar with the menus and would have memorised sequences of keypresses for the most frequently selected items. This would have reduced their mean time per menu and therefore their mean time per selection. Users of the adaptive system would have been unable to improve their performance in this way because the contents of the menus would be varying and a memorised keypress sequence might therefore select the wrong item. If this conjecture is supported then the question is whether the performance resulting from the reduction in mean search depth for the adaptive system outweighs the reduction in time per menu for the static system. And if there is an advantage then can it be justified given the extra processing requirements necessary to provide an adaptive system?

An experiment similar in design to the Greenberg and Witten study was run. Four subjects were used, each was exposed to a non adaptive and an adaptive menu system. The chief difference in the new experiment was that subjects were given 100 items to retrieve rather than the thirty eight used in the original study. The results showed that: for trials 11 to 40 performance with the adaptive system was significantly ($p < 0.01$) better than with the static system for three of the four subjects but that for trials 71 to 100 performance with the adaptive system was significantly worse ($p < 0.01$) than with the static system for two of the four subjects. The other comparisons did not reach significance. Examining the results in more detail showed that over the first thirty trials the time taken to scan individual menus was about the same for the two systems but as the sessions progressed the users of the static system were taking less time per menu. Users of the static system were therefore able to benefit from the consistency of the interface; and this improvement can be sufficient to outweigh the benefit gained by a 20% reduction in mean search depth.

The other issue examined in the Trevellyan and Browne (1987) study was that of enabling a system to swap between strategies in order to accommodate changes in the environment. Greenberg and Witten's adaptive system relies on the assumption that an individual's call pattern will approximate to the Zipf distribution. An individual who rarely calls the same number more than once will be unlikely to benefit from the changes made to menus. The solution is to introduce internal monitoring or feedback into the system so that it measures the success of its strategy. A fall-back strategy was added to the system so that the system could ensure that it performed no worse than a static system should the usage strategy fail. The first hundred calls from the primed data were used to establish a base value for the mean search depth of a static system; and the fall-back strategy was used in preference to the usage strategy if the mean search depth rose above this value.

In a second experiment four different subjects were given selection tasks with *no repeated numbers*. The "self-regulating" adaptive system used the first thirty trials to establish the mean search depth and then turned off the usage strategy because it was exceeding the base value. Comparing the adaptive system to a static system over a period of one hundred trials showed that the increase in mean search depth for the adaptive system was only 0.3%. The implication is that use of a self-regulating system can ensure that the system always performs as well as or better than a comparable static system.

Two limitations were identified in the Trevellyan and Browne work. Firstly, that the adaptive system required one hundred items of primed data. In practical circumstances this data would have to be collected during interactive use of the system, providing users with the opportunity to become adjusted to the consistent interface. Secondly, that the subjects were required to complete the task in an abnormally repetitive fashion, i.e. the task was of low fidelity as a representative scenario.

Robertson *et al.*, (1987) took up both these issues in a further set of studies. Firstly they proposed to start both systems, the adaptive and static, with no previous history. And secondly they proposed to use a longitudinal design which would approximate likely usage in an office environment.

Subjects were divided into two groups of six. Group 1 were presented with the static system first followed by the adaptive one, and Group 2 vice versa. Each subject selected 160 names per system, split over eight daily sessions. An analysis of variance with time per trial and time per menu as the dependent variables gave the following results:

For time per trial: a significant main effect for type of interface (i.e. adaptive vs static); a significant main effect for sessions; an interaction effect between sessions and order; and an interaction effect between interface type, sessions and order.

For time per menu: a significant main effect for interface type; a significant main effect for sessions; an interaction effect between interface type and order; and an interaction effect between interface type and sessions.

An ANOVA for errors per trial and errors per menu gave only one significant result: a main effect of sessions on errors per trial.

The significant main effect for interface type on both time per trial and time per menu indicated that there was a benefit due to adaptation even though the system had to build up a usage history from scratch. However, the order effect was the more interesting result, because it was unpredicted.

Further investigation of the order effect showed that time per trial was significant for Group 1 but not for Group 2. Group 1 in which the static system was presented first showed a 19.4% improvement from static to adaptive system whereas the Group 2 showed only a 0.03% improvement from static to adaptive. The means and standard deviations of time per trial across all sessions in the order and interface conditions are shown in Fig. 6.7.

An analysis of the changes in time per menu over sessions showed that as a function of being first, the adaptive system reached an asymptote on session 2, which is earlier than the static system, but by session 5 both systems were equivalent. As a function of being second, both systems showed an initial increase in time but the adaptive system provided a much earlier recovery and improvement than the static system.

Collectively, these results indicate that the type of interface presented first has an effect on performance. There was a large performance improvement when the adaptive interface was

	Session	1	2	3	4	5	6	7	8
Order 1									
Static	x̄	3.95	3.17	2.83	2.71	2.75	2.71	2.32	2.64
	sd	1.36	0.79	0.44	0.45	0.45	0.33	0.52	0.44
Adaptive	x̄	3.12	2.73	2.78	2.73	2.75	2.75	2.26	2.49
	sd	0.59	0.55	0.56	0.55	0.38	0.53	0.64	0.60
Order 2									
Adaptive	x̄	3.08	2.75	2.72	2.73	2.75	2.74	2.26	2.76
	sd	0.63	0.45	0.56	0.55	0.39	0.53	0.64	0.45
Static	x̄	3.07	3.21	3.13	2.81	2.89	3.04	2.49	2.94
	sd	0.45	0.53	0.61	0.42	0.59	0.55	0.63	0.74

Fig. 6.7 Order effect : Mean time per menu (seconds).

presented *after* the consistent interface but not when it was presented *before*. This effect was explained by proposing that presenting the consistent interface first encourages the user to develop a plan or "set" for locating names so that they can recall a sequence of keystrokes to retrieve particular alphabetic ranges of names. The memorised sequences will not work for the subsequent adaptive interface, forcing the user to abandon that strategy and resort to searching each menu. However when the adaptive system is presented first, the process of matching keystrokes with names is prevented from developing by the variation in the alphabetic subranges; this then interferes with the subsequent use of the consistent interface because users stick with the strategy of searching each menu, perhaps because they still expect the menus to vary, rather than develop the more efficient memorising strategy.

With respect to the design of adaptive computer systems the results from this study indicate:

(1) The importance of understanding the underlying task structure and hence the range of potential user strategies. The adaptive system can then be designed to substitute alternatives for one or more components of the user's

strategies. However, it is also necessary to consider the consequences for the user of such a substitution. For example in the study described, the usage strategy appeared to cause users to form a mental plan which was not compatible with the static interface.

(2) The sequence of system strategies must be considered. Even though the usage strategy in the system described looks to provide performance advantages, it should not necessarily be the first strategy presented to the user if it is anticipated that a static strategy will be invoked at some stage.

(3) The performance effect of switching between strategies needs to be taken into account. The results from the adaptive menus work show that there is a performance deficit immediately following a switch from either adaptive to static or static to adaptive strategy. There is a plausible account for this deficit: firstly the user must both recognise that the interface has changed and comprehend the change; secondly if the change is novel to the user then they must develop a new plan of interaction. The success of a strategy should therefore be judged over a sufficiently long sampling period to counteract this deficit. If switching between strategies is too rapid then overall performance will be debilitated.

To summarise: The original approach of Greenberg and Witten (1985) showed that adaptation could provide a beneficial performance effect. Further work by Trevellyan and Browne (1987) suggested that the adaptive system itself should monitor and validate the performance effect and be capable of switching between strategies in response to a changing environment. Robertson *et al.* (1987) demonstrated that there are further issues concerned with the introduction and change of strategies which have to be considered in the design of an adaptive system.

EVALUATION AND DESIGN

Finally in this chapter we look at how some of the evaluation techniques we have addressed fit into the design process as a whole.

Formative Evaluation

It has been proposed that in developing an adaptive system a method of iterative design, build and evaluation should be adopted. Checks along the way about the validity of assumptions under which the system is operating can give the designer confidence that the system will meet its objective.

User requirements analysis can be regarded as a preliminary evaluation of the needs of potential users of a system. Examination of both user requirements and the available functionality can provide an indication of potential areas for building adaptation into a system. When a potential area for adaptation has been identified the designer should describe the objective (Obj. M.) of providing this type of adaptation. Consideration should also be given at this stage to the issue of generality (Gen. M.) of the proposed adaptation, and to the parts of the niche description which describe user benefits and the likely affects of change.

The adaptation must be based on some aspect of user or task variability and a preliminary assessment of these characteristics should be undertaken. In the niche description this corresponds to the description of user characteristics in the notional world. In some cases evidence for this variability may exist in the literature but in other cases it will be necessary to carry out an empirical study. Where a theory is formulated about the relationship between the objective of the system and another aspect of user behaviour it will be necessary to describe this theory (Tass. M.).

The designer must then find an adaptive strategy which will enable the system to meet its objectives. It will be necessary therefore to identify the triggers (Trig. M.) upon which adaptation is to be based and the recommendations made in the light of these triggers (Rec. M.). The triggers and the recommendations constitute the adaptive mechanism and all aspects of the proposed adaptive mechanism should be documented at this stage. This corresponds to the description of the modelling assumptions in the niche description. It should also be possible at this stage to predict potential problems with the implementation (Imp. M.).

Summative Evaluation

Once the system has been built it will be necessary to carry out a summative or post-build evaluation. If the iterative cycle has been followed some of the post-build evaluation tests will merely serve to verify the pre-build evaluation checks. For instance the pre-build evaluation checks should have established evidence for the user variability on which the adaptation is based. The assumption that this user variability also holds in the context of the adaptive system may need to be tested as part of a summative evaluation.

The major objective of the post build evaluation of an adaptive system will usually be to establish whether the subjects' performance is better with the adaptive system than with a similar non-adaptive system. Before this question can be answered though it will be necessary to answer some preliminary questions.

The first is whether the system is actually adapting. This may involve undertaking a test such as that described earlier in which the system is forced to adapt to two mutually incompatible criteria. If the requirement is less strict, however, we can simply observe that the system is responding in pre-specified ways to pre-specified changes in input according to the theory embodied in the metrics. This may be aided by a diagnostic method such as that described previously.

The next question is whether the system is meeting the designer's objective. If the system performs as predicted under the stated assumptions then it is meeting their objective. The test for this will normally involve an experiment to determine whether or not the user's performance for a suitable task is better with the adaptive system than it is with a similar non-adaptive system. Ideally performance along the relevant dimension(s) should be measured in a within subjects design.

However, whether or not the system is able to meet the designer's objective the system may still be acceptable in a real setting. Even if the adaptive system is superior to the non- adaptive system for the measured objective, it may be that users prefer to use the non-adaptive system for other reasons. This can only be answered by performing high fidelity simulation experiments or preferably field trials. This will probably require a longitudinal study of several "representative" users using the system.

CONCLUSION

There have been some doubts expressed by human interface practitioners about the utility of adaptive systems because of the danger of having systems which change to unexpected states. This is of course a problem but it is not in itself an argument against the requirement for adaptive systems; it simply indicates that we require systems which have a dependable model, one which is both stable and comprehensible to the user. There is also little recognition of the fact that at present we have systems which, because of their inability to cope with variation, embody a set of beliefs about the world which are plainly wrong. Evaluation is one way through which it should be possible to equip systems with beliefs that are not quite so amiss!

In this chapter we have begun to tackle some of the ways in which we can ensure that adaptive interfaces are both stable and dependable and meeting their objectives. It has involved the use of a greater range of methods than might ordinarily be considered, and it has shown that the evaluation and design stages can be brought together through the early declaration of suitable measures or metrics.

Chapter 7
Conclusions

D. Browne

Previous chapters have raised as many questions concerning adaptive systems as they have answered. Discussion has included : why adaptive user interfaces are an issue for research, how can such systems be built, what techniques are available for their implementation, and how they can be evaluated? Hopefully some of the answers, or at least the complexity of the questions has been eluded to. The AID project is the largest to date to have researched the topic of Adaptive User Interfaces, but it has undoubtedly only begun the work of identifying the issues, implications, feasibility and future for such systems.

Rather than simply concluding with the virtues of adaptation; this chapter takes a more critical, look at the future. Firstly, some of the research required to speed the evolution of adaptive user interfaces is discussed. Then, some of the developments that are upon us are described. Finally, a number of the issues surrounding adaptive systems are discussed.

OUTSTANDING RESEARCH.

Progress on AID was limited by the tools and techniques available. Because of the adventurous and multi-disciplinary nature of the project most of the "burning" issues in Human-Computer Interaction were of practical concern. Task Analysis, User Modelling, Dialogue Design, Prototyping, and User Interface Separation to name but a few. For progress to be made the project had to adopt the best of the available techniques and tools.

Task Analysis.

Early in the project, Command Language Grammar (Moran, 1981) was adopted as the task analysis notation for one of our largest developments. Later in the project Checkland's (1981) soft systems methodology was felt to provide an useful task analysis aid. In retrospect neither was found to be adequate, not surprisingly, given the job for which they were designed. CLG could be used to identify design decision points, at which adaptive techniques could be employed at run-time. However, the notation suffers from being both overly repetitive, hard to maintain and lacking suitable semantics for state-of-the-art user interfaces. Checkland's soft systems methodology offers "Rich Pictures" as a means for documenting diversity. This was found useful as a means to identify possible bases for adaptation, but Rich Pictures had their deficiencies too, particularly because they are so "open" that it is difficult to identify commonalities.

While these techniques offer some support during the requirements stage of an adaptive system's development, much better techniques are required. Even for the development of non-adaptive systems, task analysis techniques and notations are inadequate and none has yet gained wide acceptance. Analysts have many techniques to choose from. The choice is probably best made on the basis of the attributes of the application. For instance, interviewing techniques may still be the best source of requirements data when building a replacement for an existing application. Repertory grid analysis may be appropriate when a knowledge based system is required. The building of adaptive systems also poses its own unique analytical needs. Techniques are required to ascertain the diversity of the user population, both in terms of individual or group differences, the tasks to be performed and the jobs to be accomplished. The AID project found no such technique readily available and had to be content with modifying existing ones.

Measuring and Modelling Users.

AID sought measures by which individuals could be distinguished. While there is an abundance of literature making claims for distinctions such as field dependence and intelligence, the difficulty is one of characterising users by such measures when the only source of data available is their interaction with the system.

Morrison and Noble (1987) quite clearly showed that measures taken through psychometric testing are correlated with performance in using a computer system. The task required interaction with a simulated database and electronic mail system. Subjects who scored better on a general intelligence test performed better (completed more tasks) with the system. Subjects rated as field independent also performed better, presumably because they were better able to deal with confusion and were better able to distinguish crucial information from background information.

Similarly Coventry (1989) found that UNIX users who were rated as field independent sought more help while field dependent users were more likely to attempt tasks of which they were unsure. The inference is that different types of help system are required for different users. But how do you identify someone as being field independent?

From this study it appears that frequency of help accessing could itself be a sufficient metric. Importantly with regard to the building of adaptive systems it may not be necessary to classify a user as field dependent/independent in order to build an appropriate model to drive adaptation. There may be sufficient data in how much help is requested.

For the most part the project attempted to build non-intrusive exemplars. That is, build systems that did not extend the dialogue purely for the purpose of user modelling. This might be considered as one of the project's biggest mistakes. Relaxing the conditions for gaining data to be used for user modelling would certainly have eased some of the problems encountered. Nonetheless, the automatic deduction of user traits/abilities must remain one of the ultimate aims of adaptive systems. For many applications it is unlikely that users will accept dialogues that have no apparent relevance to their immediate needs. Even for long-lived systems, "direct" data collection for user modelling is unlikely to be acceptable given that users adapt over time and during interaction. A well-adapted system must therefore "take soundings" during interaction and be predisposed to adapt. This was demonstrated in the work of Trevellyan and Browne (1987). An adaptive telephone directory was shown to be a feasible development but importantly it was recognised that the system's adaptation technique could not be guaranteed to work effectively. In fact, it could on occasions be maladapted to its situation and under such circumstances was more effective after having reverted to a non adaptive state. In this latter state the system could still gather data in preparation for becoming an overtly adaptive system once more.

Thus much work remains to ascertain what information can be gained from monitoring interaction for the purpose of modelling and distinguishing between users. Interactive systems cannot identify directly the cognitive processes taking place within a user. These can only be deduced from the commands issued from users, their data requests, the apparent sequence of the dialogue, timing information, errors, etc. Systems can also be made "aware" of changes in the application, such as the arrival of mail and movement in the values of data items, but precious little else. Inferences made from these two sources of data are questionable; their goodness depends on the quality of the inference engine embedded in the system. That is the rules or theory that is the mediator of adaptation. An example of this comes from one of the earliest developments on the project. An attempt was made to build a plan recogniser that could predict the tasks to be attempted by users in order that automatic support could be offered. In retrospect this objective was short-sighted. What was achieved was a tool that was found to be poor indeed, but no less successful than an independent human observer in similar circumstances. It was not that the plan recogniser was inaccurate, it was simply doomed to failure because there was insufficient information in the users' interaction to permit the required predictions to be made.

A major advance in adaptive system research will be made once a suitable model of users, with sufficient generality across a wide range of applications, is established. Even this will be inadequate if the data required by the model cannot be ascertained from user interaction. This may sound all too obvious, but far too little research is directed at identifying what can be inferred from monitoring interaction.

Briggs (1988), in a study of system use by naive users concentrated on identifying the information required for successful interaction. This was ascertained by analysing the questions posed both before and during interaction. Not surprisingly the findings demonstrated the power of preconceptions in guiding system use and that users' questions were very much goal directed and initiated by immediate task requirements. Automated system monitoring would be unlikely to make such identifications as accurately or quickly as the human observer. To do so would require the incorporation of a question answering service as an addition to the basic system. If such a service was deemed useful - and this could be ascertained from its repeat usage - then it could be a source of data for a user model.

Excepting the use of psychometric testing it is unlikely in the near or even semi-distant future that any persistent personality or cognitive traits be derived from monitoring user interaction. More hope may reside with models based on user preferences for dialogue styles, presentation formats, sequencing of tasks etc. The reason for this being that the basis for the preferences, that is the cognitive underpinnings do not need to be understood and modelled overtly. Only the utility and acceptance of the adaptations need be established. This is similar to the Skinnerian (Skinner, 1965) approach to behavioural analysis. Rather than attempt to understand the rationale and cognitive dispositions underlying behaviour, the Skinnerian approach only requires one to find out "what works". This was the approach taken in the Trevellyan & Browne (1987) and Briggs (1988) work. If sufficient measures can be found to describe what the user has done and whether the system's adaptations are useful then there is no need to understand the full complexity of why it works. Thus the likely adaptive system successes are going to be based on purely behavioural analysis rather than on theories of human cognition.

A further example is given by Mason (1986). An adaptive prompt generator was built for the UNIX Programmer's Manual application. It was found that a set of rules based on factors such as, extent of system usage, types of commands used and recency of command type usage were sufficient to provide data for purposeful adaptations that contributed to the usability of the system. This was achieved without recourse to modelling of higher level cognitive factors or enduring personality traits.

The logical conclusion of this Skinnerian view of automatic adaptation will be to use feedback to improve adaptations. Given that a system must monitor interaction in order to adapt why not build a higher level monitor that assesses the success of the adaptations with the express objective of modifying the rules/theory underlying the adaptation. Basically this would automate the role of external observer/researcher and render the adaptive system introspective and to all intents and purposes "intelligent". This would be what was referred to as "self-mediating" or possibly "self-modifying" adaptation in Chapter 3.

Another logical conclusion is to expend a lot of effort modelling users, but to do it just once and make the model highly accessible. If users are prepared to spend time being modelled then psychometric testing could be conducted with a view to generating a portable model. Norman & Draper (1986) suggest that user models be carried on 'Smart Cards'. These could then be plugged into any terminal with the effect that it offer the user an interface with which they are accustomed. Of course such a model would be mainly relevant to domain independent features of user interfaces.

User Interface Building.

Recently there has been an upsurge in the number of User Interface Management Systems coming to market. Ideally, for the building of adaptive systems, such tools should provide at least two features. Firstly, the ability to support different dialogues at run-time. That is offer the designer the flexibility to keep dialogue options open until run-time. Secondly, provide the necessary 'hooks' such that dialogue decisions be made by a user model or adaptor.

Chapter 4 discussed different types of UIMS in depth, and suggested that the "Event Driven" approach may be most applicable to the building of adaptive user interfaces. While this may be the case, no currently available UIMS adequately meets the requirements stated above.

Architecture.

The components discussed above suggest certain things about the architecture of adaptive systems. For instance, that there will be a task based modelling component, that a component be provided for user modelling and that the user interface software be uniquely identifiable. These assumptions are widely supported.

SAUCI (Tyler & Treu, 1989), includes knowledge bases for a user model, target system commands, high-level tasks and target system objects. These are not dissimilar from the components proposed by the AID project (Totterdell & Cooper 1986). The latter proposed an "application expert" holding specific knowledge bases for system commands and objects, a component known as a user model holding both user information and task specific information. Rouse *et al.* (1987) distinguish components, among others for operator modelling, adaptive aiding, error monitoring and interface management. Again many parallels can be found. These commonalities are not at all surprising, the requirements set by adaptation determine that such commonalities exist. What is important, for the future of adaptive systems, is that the basic architectural requirements be identified. By so doing, research can be directed at supporting them.

One major breakthrough may be the provision of general user modelling tools (Finin, 1989). Another may be the provision of acceptable and generally usable task description notations. When such building blocks are available, the design, implementing and testing of adaptive systems will become more feasible in terms of cost, time and risk.

Providing an adaptive interface to any system does increase the implementation complexities and cost. At present this makes adaptation prohibitively expensive for most commercial applications. As ready made components or "shells" become available these costs should decrease. Also, the computational cost of performing extensive modelling impacts system response time. Nonetheless, as hardware developments result in faster processors and lower accompanying costs this disadvantage is unlikely to be prohibitive for very long.

APPLICATIONS.

What might the impact of providing adaptive interfaces be in ten or twenty years time? Will users be accepting of technology that reacts as if imbued with the faculties of a behavioural psychologist, or a devotee of the teachings of Skinner? Answers to such questions are not yet available but some insights may be gained from consideration of recent adaptive systems applications and a little crystal ball gazing.

What should be borne in mind is that while research in the area of adaptive systems is certainly at the stage where a lot of nappy changes are still required, there can be little doubt that their graduation day will come. Unfortunately, as with all emerging technologies the developers are unlikely to consider the question of desirability as fully as might be hoped.

The following will consider some applications and how adaptive systems may impact their development. Both the positive effects and the potential negatives will be considered.

Educational Software

Surprisingly, interface design for educational software has been given little attention (Frye & Solloway, 1987). The reason for this may include the perceived lack of revenue in this domain. Nonetheless, educational software is one of the most salient application areas for the deployment of adaptive techniques. As long ago as 1959, Birmingham at the US Naval Research Laboratory built a machine controlled adaptive device to measure a human operator's ability to track high frequencies. This device adaptively changed the speed of oscillation; dependent on the operator's accuracy in tracking the frequency. This enabled Birmingham and his colleagues to measure the bandwidth of an operator's frequency tracking abilities. The elements of this system are the same as those required in adaptive training systems. To quote Kelley (1969)

"Machine controlled adaptive training has three elements: (1) a means of measuring performance, (2) an adjustable feature of the task or problem which changes its difficulty (the adaptive variable), and (3) adaptive logic which automatically changes the adaptive variable as a function of the performance measurement."

One of the attractions of adaptive educational software is the potential to educate in a well paced manner. Learners are inevitably diverse in their skill and developmental level for a domain. A trainer cannot possibly accommodate this diversity by teaching at a rate and in a sequence that best meets the requirements of each individual. At best, one can hope that the average student progresses adequately, the better equipped students are not held back and the less well equipped are not completely lost too early in a curriculum. This "one to many" teaching scenario is known to be inadequate, and this is why schools adopt streaming methods, and different categories of school exist. The most profound reaction to the problem is the establishment of remedial classes where the slow learners are helped to catch up on basic skills.

For some curricula the advent of adaptive training may be upon us. Many educational packages exist. While the quality of their user interfaces may be open to question they do offer the opportunity for individualised education. A system can offer education and test the success of recipients' interaction by using embedded tests. The results of which can then be used to adapt subsequent teaching, possibly repeating those lessons that were not so successful or increasing the pace of lessons where it is apparent that the concepts are likely to be grasped rather quickly. Unless these systems are responsive to the development level of their users then they are unlikely to be significantly better than the traditional classroom situation. The onus for adaptation will again be put back in the lap of the user, so that they actively skip lessons or repeat those that were not understood.

An adaptive educational system is being developed for the Civil Aviation Authority. "Aviation", as it is known, is designed to guide Air Traffic Control cadets through their training according to their knowledge and experience.

"...the level of intelligence that will be built into the software is what makes the system unique. It will adapt to each cadet, and store a profile of that person and their level of skill. The subject material, which will appear as computer graphics, as text or as video, will take the students through flight theory, aircraft performance and aircraft recognition." (Watts, 1988).

What are the implications of adopting such training methods as a significant part of education? The benefits may include better equipped school leavers, at least in the primary skills. Thinking positively, teachers might have more free time to apply their skills to the training of individuals in more abstract or social skills such as human interaction, politics and morality. Being cynical some may see benefits in the possibility of decreasing the number of teachers required. One pervasive question must be: How much time do we think it reasonable to have pupils, particularly the young, spend learning from interaction with an automaton? What effect might this have on the creativity of future generations? There is already a social problem caused by the attraction of computerised games. If this attraction is attributable to escapism then we ought to be concerned by the lack of reality, and experience afforded by educational software.

Aesthetics

The quality of a computer generated graphical image can be assessed against many criteria. Among the dependent factors are the task that the graphic aims to support and the preferences of the individual user. When designing a system incorporating graphics such issues are poorly addressed at present.

Holynski *et al.* (1988) have begun development of a system that takes account of task requirements and user preferences. The Adaptive Graphics Analyser (AGA) considers images in terms of a number of variables such as busyness, regularity and colour variety. By having users rate images having different attribute values, the system is able to build a model of user preferences. This model can then be used to adaptively generate images that it is believed the user will prefer. While this might seem a very intrusive and time consuming means of generating aesthetically pleasing images, it is hoped that group preferences could be elicited by sampling. In this way models could for instance, be built for architects, engineers, etc. The preliminary version of AGA is being used to create screen displays and iconic menu options for educational software.

A genuine worry regarding adaptive techniques arises when consideration is given to their effect if employed in creative applications. It is questionable whether the artist within us will be facilitated by an automaton, especially if the automaton is guided by a model of us.

Open Systems

One of the most talked about topics in the computer world at present is Open Systems Interconnection (OSI). Essentially this refers to the connection of diverse systems permitting intercommunication. A standard to be applied when developing new systems, called the ISO seven layer communications architecture protocol (Tanenbaum, 1989), aims to provide an agreed basis upon which OSI can be achieved.

It is a mouth-watering thought for many individuals and organisations that at some future date access to a magnitude more functionality will be available from a single point. But at what price? Each node in the network of an open system may have a unique operating system, and thus command language, syntax and specialist devices ie. for hardcopy production. To make full use of "openness" the user will be required to learn and remember far more than ever before.

"...the differences may be subtle, or so fundamental that the user may not be able to use the new system at all, may use it destructively or may develop bad habits that could impair his use of the original system." (Hannemyr 1983).

The ultimate idea is that anyone should be able to access and utilise any of the facilities available from a single point. Thus functionality would be offered to an even wider user population than ever before. As Chapter 2 pointed out, increasing the range of users also widens the requirements placed on a system.

"Certain groups of users will require a verbose and self-prompting system to access a small range of simple services (eg bulletin boards, file transfers); while others may demand a terse and transparent system giving access to advanced facilities...." (Hannemyr, 1983).

The most salient solution to this prospective problem would be to standardize interaction dialogues. The emergence of standards such as Common User Access (CUA) (International Business Machines, 1987) may be a reaction to this need and be seen as a solution. A number of issues relating to standardisation are worth noting. Firstly, any standard always runs the risk of limiting the resulting system in some undesirable manner. Such limitations may render the system less attractive than one that breaks the standard. Secondly, standards rarely resolve or offer answers at every option. For instance, no standard can hope to, or should attempt to determine the names of commands for particular applications or the content of every error message. Thirdly, taken to the extreme, standards imply homogeneity and correctness. That is, if a standard is followed then it will be to the good of all. The subject matter of this book does not share the sentiment that user interfaces be standardised.

While the low level components of the ISO model may as well conform there are arguments against standardising the user interface of Open systems. Alternative or adaptive user interfaces may be required for Open systems to gain wide acceptance without alienating many users. Thus, adaptive user interfacing may afford a means whereby a heterogeneous user population can obtain the benefits of OSI without suffering the shortcomings of standardised user interfaces. Nonetheless, problems may arise in such a scenario. For instance, how would a help desk be able to respond to an individual's on-line problems. The individualised or even idiosyncratic nature of one person's adaptive interface might be rather difficult to convey to a central resource dealing with hundreds of users.

Adaptation In Space

As ever, the military and space industries may be the pathfinders. An adaptive system has already been prototyped for operation in space (Alexander *et al.*, 1986). The Columbus Space Station being developed by the European Space Agency is intended to be connected to the United States Space Station to form a long-term manned platform. Included on the platform will be a Crew Work Station (CWS) offering access to numerous services ranging from word processing to experiment specific applications.

Given that the end-users of this workstation will vary in terms of skills, training and task requirements the provision of an adaptive user interface seems laudable. For instance, users could be flight commanders, payload specialists, etc.; they could have just joined the space station or be finishing their tour of duty after many hours of interaction at the workstation; each crew member will have different responsibilities, interests and goals; their training could be as diverse as engineering and biology, and factors such as zero gravity will have their own effects.

Using knowledge-based techniques together with a task model, and user model representing skills, knowledge, aims and responsibilities of individuals, the CWS will provide an adaptively controlled information display. Among the facilities to be adapted are the help, explanation, and tutorials provided. These will be adapted on the basis of rules embedded in the software and information held in knowledge bases.

It is hoped that such a system could facilitate interaction in situations where crew members fall ill and their duties are conducted by a replacement. When crew members first arrive the system will be responsive to their lack of hands-on experience, and as users get more skilled the user interface will adapt with them.

Rouse et al., (1987-8), developed a prototype system with an adaptive component for application to fighter aircraft operations. The goal is for the fighter pilot to remain in control at all times but be provided with a system that adapts to current needs and capabilities. In this way human and computer resources can be utilised optimally, enhancing overall performance. The pilot's state is modelled in terms of:

activities - what is the pilot currently doing or likely to be doing?

awareness - what task requirements is the pilot conscious of?

intentions - what are the pilots goals and plans?

resources - what human information processing and interaction resources are available?

performance - how well is the pilot performing or likely to perform?

One of the main adaptations invoked by the system is task allocation. On the basis of the pilot's state, system state and world state, tasks or parts of tasks might be undertaken by the computer on behalf of the pilot. For instance, flight control might be divided into lateral and longitudinal with the former being performed by the computer. Feedback in terms of performance measures are used by the system to assess how adaptation should progress. Following an adaptation, if performance improvements are not as expected then further task re-allocation may be performed.

OUTSTANDING RESEARCH ISSUES

Hunting

Many undesirable side-effects of providing adaptive systems can be thought of. In the same manner that poorly designed non-adaptive systems can be built, possibly even greater potential, for building poor adaptive systems exists. One of the main worries has been referred to as hunting. This can occur when the adaptive system is trying to establish a user model and the user is trying to establish a system model (Gaines & Shaw, 1983). While these two models are in a state of flux no opportunity exists for a stable state to be reached.

To compensate for this it has been suggested that the user be given an explicit model of the adaptations being undertaken by the system. For instance, the user may be notified that the position of items on a menu may change according to their most frequent choices, or that tests will be repeated when success falls below a given level. In this way the user can anticipate, or at least rationalise the actions being taken by the system.

Lack of Control

Norcio & Stanley (1988), point out that a major negative might be the user's feeling of lack of control. Wahlster & Kobsa (1986) have pointed out that users may even attempt to disguise their goals and preferences. To ameliorate this possibility they suggest that users be given an inspectable version of the system's user model. A further alternative is to give the user the "Red Button" option. That is, allow them to turn off adaptation. In this way they are being given ultimate control, the knowledge of which may be sufficient for them to be accepting of the adaptations.

Pigeonholing

Imagine the jet setting business woman who runs her own international business. Each time she wishes to book a flight the same set of questions need to be answered. "Smoking or Non-smoking Madam?" " Would you like an aisle or a window seat?" " Would Madam prefer to sit in economy or business class?" By carrying a smart card with all such details stored magnetically then the whole process could be speeded significantly. The only question required would be, "Would Madam like to travel in the manner to which She is accustomed?" The particular user attributes that are required for a specific adaptive system will tend to "pigeonhole" users. in a more selective and comprehensive way than has been employed hitherto.

Data Protection

The most emotive argument against Adaptive systems may be that people do not want machines holding their personal data. This may become a major issue depending on how such information is used. For instance, an electronic mail order catalogue system may offer each user a personalised set of purchase options. A scenario could be generated whereby mail ordering becomes a more interactive and personalised process. The system affords you the opportunity to devise situations from which it can help you identify a purchase. For instance, you wish to purchase an item of "object d'art" for your great aunt whose birthday is approaching. The system helps you in this endeavour and Aunt Nellie receives a much appreciated salad bowl. Next year at a similar time the system opens a dialogue with you once more, but this time it is on the "offensive" (excuse the anthropomorphism). It is armed with more information. Aunt Nellie is known to have a birthday nearing, and she is the proud owner of a salad bowl. How about buying Auntie the new range of cut glass salad spoons to match the bowl? Before you know it you are sold. This may have eased your problems of present buying but how would you feel about a mere automaton knowing the date of your Aunt's birthday, or even what she has sitting on her living room table.

Information has been gathered in the process of using a model and you have to live with it.

Benefits

The anticipated benefits of adaptive systems are numerous at the individual, group and society levels. Possible benefits being different depending on the application. For instance, in a workshop application individuals could be more satisfied during their working hours, while in a military application a so-called benefit might be that a country is better defended. A few possible high-level benefits are briefly mentioned, below.

The work of Rouse *et al.* (1987-8) described earlier, provides a good example of how adaptive techniques might be employed to support task allocation. Depending on variables such as world state and user state a system can determine whether to perform tasks on behalf of the user. It can be hoped that such techniques be employed in many application areas in order to improve the satisfaction gained from performing a job of work. Rather than a user be stressed by the pressures of work or bored by repetitive and mundane tasks the system could adapt in order to enhance the quality of work.

Adaptive techniques might also be employed to pace work and encourage users to attempt more exacting endeavours. Some systems are now so diverse in their capabilities that individuals only ever experience a small percentage of those systems' capabilities. This appears to occur because users can simply "get by" with what they have learned thus far without needing to investigate possibly faster and more rewarding means of utilising the system. By introducing users to those as yet unknown facilities, at judiciously chosen moments, adaptive systems could broaden the proficiency of many users.

As happened in the industrial revolution, the information technology revolution could result in a loss of identity for many workers. When many people are employed to the same ends in a factory like situation the scope for expressing one's individuality and for being recognised on one's merits can be limited. It is at least conceptually feasible that adaptive techniques be employed to ameliorate such a scenario and ensure that everyone is treated as an individual.

"Rather than be locked into so-called 'user-friendly' but too often unchallenging and simple-minded interface designs that thwart creativity and indeed lead to disenchantment with technology, those many office workers can be provided the 'context' at the interface which will adaptively and gently nurture them along toward much more meaningful and useful understanding of what computers can do." (Tyler & Treu, 1989).

CONCLUSIONS

A computer is useful if its behaviour corresponds to the needs of its users. Computers operate in a world which is dynamic and diverse. Consequently, the computer needs to recognise and track the varying contingenicies it is placed under, interpret those contingencies, respond accordingly and then evaluate the effects of its behaviour. Behaviour is negotiated between the computer and its world via an interface. An adaptive interface is an interface which remains well designed even as its world changes. That is our understanding of an adaptive computer interface.

An adaptive interface is in some part an extended guarantee against obsolescence. By giving the computer an internal representation of its world it is empowered to maintain itself over a wider range of external changes. Without it the computer's behaviour will only be useful whilst its world is the same or whilst the world is willing to make itself look the same. Our argument then is not about whether adaptive interfaces are a goodthing or not. Adaptation is not a magical component which can be slottedin alongside widget X. Instead it is the rationale for the design of increasingly complex behavioural systems, which is what computers are. In particular it is the rationale for the design of highly interactive systems, hence the emphasis on the interface. Why build a more complex interactive system unless by doing so that system is better able to cope with the complexity of the things with which it interacts?

However, as well as trying to represent this general view of adaptive interface design we have also tried to show that there are some very tangible consequences concomitant with the design and building of adaptive interfaces. We have shown, for example, that to design interfaces which accommodate the heterogeneity rather than the homogeneity of users, requires new design methods, new evaluation methods and new tools. We have also shown that some current techniques, current models and current systems from human-computer interaction also have their part to play. And importantly we have also demonstrated that the interface does not always need a complex model of its users in order to improve its performance. This should help provide a stepping stone for the construction of new adaptive interfaces.

Hopefully, too, we have shown that there are some socially desirable features of adaptive interfaces. For example, adaptive interfaces give recognition to the fact that not everyone is the same but that everyone develops. We have also indicated a potentially wide market for adaptive interface technology. But all this we have tempered with the recognition that adaptive interfaces are not without their problems. Problems in commissioning because of the initial cost of R & D. Problems in design such as the narrow bandwidth of communication between user and interface. And potential problems in use such as unpredictability, hunting behaviour,and intrusiveness. Proactive initiatives will need to be taken to manage the impact of adaptive interface technology, particularly with regard to user modelling and the use of personal data.

Regrettably, at present it is far easier for designers to ignore diversity and treat similar things as being the same. Users are users are users with no qualifications. However, when methods are used which make explicit the benefits of adaptation and the cost of achieving those benefits are reduced then we will begin to see adaptive interfaces have an impact on information technology. It is to be expected that adaptation will be instrumental in the construction of well designed interactive systems. It should be remembered, however, that there are presently many inadequacies in the design of interactive systems which will also need resolving before we can confidently devise technological artefacts which are both useful and usable..

References

Adhami, E. and Browne, D. P. (1987) Generic user interfaces to multiple applications. *Third International Expert Systems Conference*, pp. 233–244. Learned Information, London.

Alexander, I., Morrisroe, G., Norris, P. and Tindell, A. (1986) Human factors in the Columbus Space Station. In Harrison, M. D. and Monk, A. F. (eds), *People and Computers: Designing for Usability*, pp. 97–114. Cambridge University Press, Cambridge.

Alty, J. L. (1984a) Use of path algebras in an interactive adaptive dialogue system. In Shackel, B. (ed.), *INTERACT '84*, pp. 321–324. Elsevier, Amsterdam.

Alty, J. L. (1984b) The application of path algebras to interactive dialogue design. *Behaviour and Information Technology* 3(2), 119–132.

Alty, J. L. and McKell, P. (1986) Application modelling in a User Interface Management System. In Harrison, M. and Monk, A. (eds), *People and Computers: Designing for Usability*, pp. 319–335. Cambridge University Press, Cambridge.

Anderson, S. (1987) *Context in Adaptive Systems*. International AID report.

Arbib, M. A. (1972) *The Metaphorical Brain*. Wiley-Interscience, New York.

Axelrod, R. (1984) *The Evolution of Cooperation*. Basic Books.

Backhouse, R. C. and Carre, B. A. (1975) Regular algebra applied to path finding problems. *Journal of the Institute of Mathematics and its Application* 15, 161–186.

Barnard, P. J., Hammond, N. V., McLean, A. and Morton, J. (1982) Learning and remembering interactive commands in a text-editing task. *Behaviour and Information Technology* 1(4), 437–458.

Barwise, J. and Perry, J. (1983) *Situations and attitudes*. MIT Press, Cambridge, MA.

Bechtel, W. (1985) Realism, instrumentalism and the intentional stance. *Cognitive Science* 9, 473–497.

Bennett, J. L. (1976) User-oriented graphics system for decision support in unstructured tasks. ACM/SIGGRAPH Workshop on User-oriented Design of Interactive Graphics Systems.

Benyon, D. (1984) Monitor—a self adaptive interface. In Shackel, B. (ed.), *INTERACT '84*. Elsevier, Amsterdam.

Berry, D. C. and Broadbent, D. E. (1984) On the relationship between task performance and associated verbalisable knowledge. *Quarterly Journal of Experimental Psychology* 36A, 209–231.

Birmingham, H. P. (1959) The instantaneous measurement of human operator bandwidth. *Eighth Annual Conference on Manual Control*. Dun Lap and associates incorporated, Stamford, CT.

Boyle, E. (1988) The evaluation of adaptive systems. Internal AID Report. aid/3/report/m0080.1

Briggs, P. (1988) What we know and what we need to know: the user model versus the user's model in human–computer interaction. *Behaviour and Information Technology* **7**(4), 431–442.

Brooks, A. and Alty, J. L. (1985) The use of rule induction. In Johnson, P. and Cook, S. (eds), *People and Computers: Designing the Interface*. Cambridge University Press, Cambridge.

Browne, D. P. (1987) *Man–Machine Interfaces for Intelligent Knowledge Based Systems*. IEE Colloquium Digest No: 1987/107, 2/1–2/3.

Browne, D. P., Sharratt, B. D. and Norman, M. A. (1986) The formal specification of adaptive user interfaces using command language grammar. *Proceedings of the Conference on Human Factors in Computing Systems, Boston, Massachusetts*, pp. 256–260.

Browne, D. P., Trevellyan, R., Totterdell, P. A. and Norman, M. (1987) Metrics for the building, evaluation and comprehension of self-regulating adaptive systems. In Bullinger, H. J. and Shackel, B. (eds), *INTERACT '87*. Elsevier-North Holland, Amsterdam.

Buie, E. A. (1986) Bibliography: individual differences and computer–human interaction. ACM SIGCHI Bulletin, pp. 47–49.

Bundy, A. (1984) Intelligent front ends. Pergamon Infotech State of the Art Report *Expert Systems*. Pergamon Infotech.

Bury, K. F., Boyle, J. M., Evey, R. J. and Neal, A. S. (1982) Windowing versus scrolling on a visual display terminal. *Human Factors*, **24**(4), 385–394.

Carre, B. A. (1971) An algebra for network routing problems. *Journal of the Institute of Mathematics and its Application* **7**, 273–294.

Carroll, J. M. and McKendree, J. (1987) Interface design issues for advice-giving expert systems. *Communications of the ACM* **30**(1), 14–31.

Carroll, J. M. and Thomas, J. C. (1980) Metaphor and the cognitive representation of computing systems. IBM Watson Research Centre, Research Report RC8302 (No. 35942).

Chase, W. G. and Simon, H. A. (1973) Perception in chess. *Cognitive Psychology* **4**, 55–81.

Checkland, P. B. (1981) *Systems Thinking, Systems Practice*. Wiley, Chichester.

Clowes, I. (1988) Methodology for designing adaptive user interfaces. Internal AID Report. aid/2.41/concept/s0111.3

Clowes, I., Cole, I., Arshad, F., Hopkins, C. and Hockley, A. (1985) User modelling techniques. In Johnson, P. and Cook, S. (eds) *People and Computers: Designing the Interface*, pp. 35–45. Cambridge University Press, Cambridge.

Cohill, A. M. and Williges, R. C. (1982) Computer-augmented retrieval of HELP information for novice users. *Proceedings of the Human Factors—26th Annual Meeting*, pp. 79–82.

Coventry, L. (1989) Some effects of cognitive style on learning UNIX. *International Journal of Man–Machine Studies* **31**(3), 349–363.

Croft, W. B. (1984) The role of context and adaptation in user interfaces. *International Journal of Man–Machine Studies* **21**, 283–292.

Damereau, F. J. (1964) A technique for computer detection and correction of spelling errors. *Communications of the ACM* **6**, 171–176.

Daniels, P. J. (1986) Cognitive models in information retrieval—an evaluative review. *Journal of Documentation* **42**(4), 272–304.

DeJong, K. A. (1980) Adaptive system design: a genetic approach. *IEEE Transactions on System, Man and Cybernetics* **10**(9), 566–574.

Dennet, D. C. (1978) *Brainstorms*. Bradford Books, Montgomery.

Douglas, S. (1987) Context and user models. CHI '87 Workshop on User Models.

Dumais, S. T. and Landauer, T. K. (1982). Psychological investigations of natural terminology for command and query languages. In Badre, A. and Scheiderman, B. (eds), *Directions in Human/Computer Interaction*, pp. 95–109. Ablex, Norwood, New Jersey.

Edmonds, E. A. (1981) Adaptive man–computer interfaces. In Coombs, H. J. and Alty, J. L. (eds), *Computing Skills and the User Interface*. Academic Press, London.

Edmonds, E. A. (1982) The man–computer interface: a note on concepts and design. *International Journal of Man–Machine Studies* **16**, 231–236.

Edmonds, E. A. and Guest, S. (1978) SYNICS—a Fortran subroutine package for translation. Man–Computer Interaction Research Report No. 6, Leicester Polytechnic.

Egan, D. E. and Gomez, L. M. (1982) Characteristics of people who can learn to use computer text editors: hints for future text editor design and training. *Proceedings of the ASIS Annual Meeting 19*, pp. 75–79.

Finin, T. W. (1989) GUMS—a general user modeling shell. In Kobsa, A. and Wahlster, W. (eds), *User Models in Dialog Systems*, pp. 411–431. Springer-Verlag, New York.

Flecchia, M. A. and Bergeron, R. D. (1987) Specifying complex dialogs in ALGAE. CHI + GI '87. Conference Proceedings: Human Factors in Computing Systems and Graphics interface, pp. 229–234.

Fleishman, E. A. and Quaintance, M. K. (1984) *Taxonomies of Human Performance, The Description of Human Tasks*. Academic Press, London.

Forsyth, R. S. (1987) The evolution of intelligence. *Proceedings Third International Expert Systems Conference*. Learned Information, Oxford.

Fowler, C. J. H., Macaulay, L. A. and Fowler, J. F. (1985) The relationship between cognitive style and dialogue style: an explorative study. In Johnson, P. and Cook, S. (eds) *People and Computers: Designing the Interface*, pp. 186–198. Cambridge University Press, Cambridge.

Friend, J. (1987) Adaptive interactive spelling corrector. Internal AID Report aid/2/report/d0101.1.

Frye, D. and Soloway, E. (1987) Interface design: a neglected issue in educational software. CHI + GI '87. *Conference Proceedings of Human Factors in Computing Systems and Graphics Interface*, pp. 93–97.

Fullan, M. and Loubser, J. J. (1972) Education and adaptive capacity. *Sociology of Education* **45**, 271–287.

Furnas, G. W. (1985) Experience with an adaptive indexing scheme. *Proceedings CHI*, pp. 131–135.

Gaines, B. R. (1972) Axioms for adaptive behaviour. *International Journal of Man–Machine Studies*, **4**, 169–197.

Gaines, B. and Shaw, M. L. (1983) Dialog engineering. In Sime, M. E. and Coombs, M. J. (eds), *Designing for Human–Computer Communication*, pp. 23–53. Academic Press, London.

Gargan, R. A., Sullivan, J. W. and Tyler, S. W. (1988) Multimodal response planning: an adaptive rule based approach. CHI '88 Conference Proceedings of Human Factors in Computing Systems, pp. 229–234.

Goldstein, I. P. (1982) The genetic graph: a representation for the evolution of procedural knowledge. In Sleeman, D. and Brown, J. S. (eds) *Intelligent Tutoring Systems*, pp. 51–77. Academic Press, London.

Gould, J. D., Boies, S. J., Levy, S., Richards, J. T. and Schoonard, J. (1987) The 1984 Olympic Message System: a test of behavioral principles of system design. *Communications of the ACM* **30**, 758–769.

Green, M. (1984) Report on dialogue specification tools. *Computer Graphics Forum* **3**, 305–313.

Green, M. (1986) A survey of three dialogue models. *ACM Transactions on Graphics* **5**(3), 244–275.

Greenberg, S. (1984) User modelling in interactive computer systems. MSc thesis, Department of Computer Science, University of Calgary.

Greenberg, S. and Witten, I. H. (1985) Adaptive personalised interfaces—a question of viability. *Behaviour and Information Technology* **4**(1), 31–45.

Grosz, B. J. (1977) The representation and use of focus in dialogue understanding. PhD thesis, University of California.

Grune, D. and Jacobs, C. J. H. (1988) A Programmer-friendly LL(1) parser generator. *Software-Practise and Experience* **18**(1), 29–38.

Guest, S. P. (1982) The use of software tools for dialogue design. *International Journal of Man–Machine Studies* **16**, 263–285.

Gunning, R. (1959) *How to Take the Fog Out of Writing*. Dartnell Press, Chicago.

Hannemyr, G. (1983) Human-factors standards. The design of conceptual language interfaces to open computer network application and management systems. *Behaviour and Information Technology* **2**(4), 345–356.

Harel, D. (1988) On Visual Formalisms. *Communications of the ACM* **31**(5), 514–531.

Hetteman, P. (1979) *Personality and Adaptation*. North Holland, Amsterdam.

Hewett, T. T. (1986) The role of evaluation in designing systems for usability. In Harrison, M. D. and Monk, A. F. (eds) *People and Computers: Designing for Usability*, pp. 196–214. Cambridge University Press, Cambridge.

Hildebrant, G. and Moog, R. (1988) Mechanisms of circadian adaptation. *Acta Physiologica Polonica* **39**(5–6), 326–344.

Hill, R. D. (1986) Supporting concurrency, communication and synchronization in human–computer interaction—the Sassafras UIMS. *ACM Transactions on Graphics* **5**(3), 179–210.

Hill, R. D. (1987) Event-response systems—a technique for representing multi-threaded dialogues. *Conference Proceedings of Human Factors in Computing Systems and Graphics Interface*, pp. 241–248.

Hockley, A. (1986) Adaptive user interfaces for information systems: an evaluation. *Fourth Symposium on Empirical Foundations of Information and Software Sciences*.

Holland, J. H. (1984) Genetic algorithms and adaptation. In Selfridge, O. G., Rissland, E. L. and Arib, M. A. (eds) *Adaptive Control of Ill-Defined Systems*, pp. 317–333. Plenum Press, New York.

Holynski, M. (1988) User-adaptive computer graphics. *International Journal of Man–Machine Studies* **29**(5), 539–548.

Hoppe, H. U. (1988) Task-oriented parsing—a diagnostic method to be used by adaptive systems. *CHI '88 Conference Proceedings of Human Factors in Computing Systems*, pp. 241–248.

Howard, S. and Murray, D. M. (1987) A taxonomy of evaluation techniques for H.C.I. In Bullinger, H. J. and Shackel, B. (eds), *INTERACT '87*, pp. 453–459. Elsevier-North Holland, Amsterdam.

Innocent, P. R. (1982) Towards self-adaptive interface systems. *International Journal of Man–Machine Studies* **16**, 287–299.

International Business Machines (1987) Systems application architecture. Common user access. Panel design and user interaction. SC26-4351-0.

Jerrams-Smith, J. (1985) SUSI—a smart user-system interface. In Johnson, P. and Cook, S. (eds) *People and Computers: Designing the Interface,* pp. 211–220. Cambridge University Press, Cambridge.

Johnson, P. (1985) Toward a task model of messaging: an example of the application of TAKD to user interface design. In Johnson, P. and Cook, S. (eds), *People and Computers: Designing the Interface,* pp. 46–62. Cambridge University Press, Cambridge.

Johnson, P., Johnson, H., Waddington, R. and Shouls, A. (1988) Task-related knowledge structures: analysis, modelling and application. *Proceedings HCI '88.*

Kamran, A. (1985) Issues pertaining to the design of a user interface management system. In Pfaff, G. E. (ed.), *User Interface Management Systems.* Springer-Verlag, New York.

Kamran, A. and Feldman, M. B. (1983) Graphics programming Independent of Interaction techniques and styles. *ACM Computer Graphics* **17**(1), 58–66.

Kass, R. and Finin, T. (1988) A general user modelling facility. CHI '88 *Proceedings of the Conference on Human Factors in Computing Systems,* pp. 145–150.

Keane, M. and Johnson, P. (1987) Preliminary analysis for design. In Diaper, D. and Winder, R. (eds), *People and Computers III,* pp. 135–146. Cambridge University Press, Cambridge.

Kelley, C. R. (1969) What is adaptive training? *Human Factors* **11**(6), 547–556.

Kelly, G. A. (1955) *The Psychology of Personal Constructs.* Norton, New York.

Kemp, N. J. and Clegg, C. W. (1987) Information technology and job design: a case study on computerized numerically controlled machine tool working. *Behaviour and Information Technology* **6**(2), 109–124.

Koeffler, R. P. (1986) Classifying users: a hard look at some controversial issues. *ACM SIGCHI Bulletin* **18**(2), 75–76.

Larkin, J. H., Reif, F., Carbonell, J. and Gugliotta, A. (1988) FERMI: a flexible expert reasoner with multi-domain inferencing. *Cognitive Science* **12**(1), 101–138.

Lawson, B. R. (1979) Cognitive strategies in architectural design. *Ergonomics* **22**(1), 59–68.

Leiser, P., Mayes, T. and McEachen, P. (1988) Evaluation of adaptive menu defaults. Internal AID Report aid/3/report/m0084.1.

Levine, S. H., Goodenough-Trepagnier, C., Rosen, M. I. and Getschow, C. O. (1986) Adaptive technique for customised interface design with application to nonvocal communication. Proceedings of the RESNA 9th Annual Conference, Minneapolis, Minnesota.

Lewis, D. (1972) General semantics. In Davidson, D. and Harman, G. H. (eds), *Semantics of Natural Language.* Reidel, Dodrecht.

Mackay, C. (1984) Psychological factors in the breakdown of human adaptation. In Cullen, J. and Siegrist, J. (eds) *Psychological and Sociological Parameters for Studies of Breakdown in Human Adaptation.* Martinus Nijhoff.

Maguire, M. (1982) An evaluation of published recommendations on the design of man–computer dialogues. *International Journal of Man–Machine Studies* **16**, 237–261.

Malone, T. B., Kirkpatrick, M. and Heasly, C. (1984) Human computer interface effectiveness evaluation. In Shackel, B. (ed.) *INTERACT '84*. Elsevier-North Holland, Amsterdam.

Martens, H. H. (1959) Two notes on machine learning. *Information Control* **2**, pp. 364–379.

Maskery, H. S. (1984) Adaptive interfaces for naive users—an experimental study. In Shackel, B. (ed.), *INTERACT '84*. Elsevier-North Holland, Amsterdam.

Mason, M. V. (1986) Adaptive command prompting on an on-line documentation system. *International Journal of Man–Machine Studies* **25**(1), 33–52.

Mason, M. V. and Thomas, R. C. (1984) Experimental adaptive interface. *Information Technology* **3**(3), 162–167.

Maude, T. I., Heaton, N. O., Gilbert, G. N., Wilson, P. A. and Marshall, C. J. (1984) An experiment in group working on mailbox systems. In Shackel, B. (ed.), *INTERACT '84*, pp. 396–400. Elsevier-North Holland, Amsterdam.

Maynard Smith, J. (1985) *Evolution and the Theory of Games*. Cambridge University Press, Cambridge.

Maynard Smith, J. (1986) The evolution of animal intelligence. In Hookway, C. (ed.), *Mind, Machines and Evolution*. Cambridge University Press, Cambridge.

Michalski, R. S., Carbonell, J. G. and Mitchell, T. M. (1986) *Machine Learning*, vol. II. Morgan Kaufman, Los Altos.

Miyake, N. (1982) Constructive interaction. Technical Report No. 113. San Diego: University of California, Center for Human Information processing.

Moran, T. P. (1981) The command language grammar: a representation for the user interface of interactive computer systems. *International Journal of Man–Machine Studies* **15**, 3–50.

Moran, T. P. (1983) Getting into a system: external–internal task mapping analysis. Proceedings CHI '83 Human Factors in Computing Systems, ACM, New York, pp. 45–49.

Morland, D. V. (1983) Human factors guidelines for terminal interface design. *Communications of the ACM* **26**(7), 484–494.

Morrison, P. R. and Noble, G. (1987) Individual differences and ergonomic factors in performance on a videotex-type task. *Behaviour and Information Technology* **1**, 69–88.

Myers, B. and Buxton, W. (1986) Creating highly-interactive and graphical user interfaces by demonstration. *ACM Computer Graphics* **20**(4), 249–258.

Naur, P. (1963) Revised report on the algorithmic language Algol. *Communications of the ACM* **6**, 1–17.

Nickerson, R. S. (1981) Why interactive computer systems are sometimes not used by people who might benefit from them. *International Journal of Man–Machine Studies* **15**, 469–483.

Noah, W. H. and Halpin, S. M. (1986) Adaptive user interfaces for planning and decision aids in C3I systems. *IEEE Transactions on Systems, Man, and Cybernetics* **16**(6), 909–918.

Norcio, A. F. and Stanley, J. (1988) Adaptive human–computer interfaces. Naval Research Laboratory Report 9148.

Norman, D. A. and Draper, S. W. (eds) (1986) *User Centered System Design: New Perspectives on Human Computer Interaction.* Erlbaum, Hillsdale, New Jersey.

Ogborn, J. M. and Johnson, L. (1982) Conversation theory. Internal Report of Man Computer Studies Group, Brunel University.

Olsen, D. R. (1986) MIKE: the menu kontrol environment. *ACM Transactions on Graphics* **5**(4), 318–344.

Olsen, D. R. and Dance, J. R. (1988) Macros by example in a graphical UIMS. *IEEE Computer Graphics and Applications* **8**(1), 68–78.

Olsen, D. R. and Dempsey, E. P. (1983) SYNGRAPH: a graphical user interface generator. *ACM Computer Graphics* **17**(3), 43–50.

O'Malley, C. O., Draper, S. W. and Riley, M. S. (1984) Constructive interaction: a method for studying user–computer–user interaction. In Shackel, B. (ed.), *INTERACT '84.* Elsevier-North Holland, Amsterdam.

Payne, S. J. (1984) Task-action grammars. In Shackel, B. (ed.), *INTERACT '84*, pp. 139–144. Elsevier-North Holland, Amsterdam.

Payne, S. J. and Green, T. R. (1983) Task-action grammars—a model of the mental representation of task languages. *Human Computer Interaction* **2**, 93–133.

Piaget, J. (1955) *The Language and Thought of the Child.* New York Modern Library, New York.

Pickering, J. A., Arnott, J. L., Wolff, J. G. and Swiffin, A. L. (1984) Prediction and adaption in a communication aid for the disabled. In Shackel, B. (ed.), *INTERACT '84.* Elsevier-North Holland, Amsterdam.

Polson, P. G., Bovair, S. and Kieras, D. (1987) Transfer between text editors. *CHI + GI Conference Proceedings Human factors in Computing Systems and Graphics Systems*, pp. 27–32.

Probert, D. (1984) Intelligent front-ends—opportunities, edited highlights from the Joint Alvey MMI/IKBS Workshop on Applications Driven Research. Available from the Alvey Directorate, Millbank Tower, London.

Pylyshyn, Z. W. (1984) Computation and Cognition. Bradford Books, MIT Press, Cambridge, MA.

Rautenbach, P. (1988) Evaluation of adaptive menu defaults. Internal AID Report aid/3/design/s0225.1.

Rautenbach, P., Anderson, S., Wilkinson, A. and Totterdell, P. (1988) Adaptive user interface techniques. Internal AID Report aid/3/report/s0232.1.

Reisner, P. (1981) Formal grammar and human factors design of an interactive graphics system. *IEEE Transactions on Software Engineering* **7**(2), 229–240.

Rich, E. A. (1979) Building and exploiting user models. PhD Thesis, Carnegie Mellon University.

Rich, C. and Waters, R. C. (1982) The disciplined use of simplifying assumptions. *ACM SIGSOFT Softward Engineering Notes* **7**(5), 150.

Riches, D. S. (1988) Methodology for adaptive interface design. Internal AID Report aid/3/report/e0152.2.

Robertson, C., Thornton, M. and Norman, M. (1987) Adaptive menu defaults—a test of equivalence. Internal AID Report aid/2/report/h006.1.

Roemer, J. M. and Chapanis, A. (1982) Learning performance and attitudes as a function of the reading level of a computer-presented tutorial. In *Proceedings of the Human Factors in Computing Systems Conference*, pp. 239–244. ACM, New York.

Rosson, M. B. (1984) The role of experience in editing. In Shackel, B. (ed.), *INTERACT '84*, pp. 225–230. Elsevier-North Holland, Amsterdam.

Rothliesberger, F. J. and Dickson, W. J. (1939) *Management and the Worker: An Account of a Research Program Conducted by the Western Electric Company.* Harvard University Press, Chicago.

Rouse, W. B., Geddes, N. D. and Curry, R. E. (1987) An architecture for intelligent interfaces: outline of an approach to supporting operators of complex systems. *Human–Computer Interaction* **3**(2), 87–122.

Savory, S. (1986) What is an explanation. KBS '86, Knowledge Based Systems, pp. 231–238.

Schneider, M. L. (1982) Models for the design of static software user assistance. In Badre, A. and Schneiderman, B. (eds), *Direction in Human/Computer Interaction*, pp. 131–148. Ablex, Norwood, New Jersey.

Schneiderman, B. (1979) Human factors in computer and information systems. *IEEE Computer* **12**(12), 9–20.

Schneiderman, B. (1982) Multiparty grammars and related features for defining interactive systems. *IEEE Transactions on Systems, Man, and Cybernetics* **12**(2), 148–154.

Scott, M. L. and Yap, S. (1988) A Grammar-based approach to the automatic generation of user–interface dialogues. CHI '88 Conference Proceedings Human Factors in Computing Systems, pp. 73–78.

Scriven, M. (1972) The methodology of evaluation. In Tyler, R., Gagne, R. and Scriven, M. (eds), *Perspectives in Curriculum Evaluation*. Rand McNally, Chicago.

Selfridge, O. G. (1984) Some themes and primitives in ill-defined systems. In Selfridge, O. G., Rissland, E. L. and Arbib, M. A. (eds), *Adaptive Control of Ill-Defined Systems*. Plenum Press, New York.

Shackel, B. (1986) Ergonomics in design for usability. In Harrison, M. D. and Monk, A. F. (eds), *People and Computers: Designing for Usability*, pp. 44–64. Cambridge University Press, Cambridge.

Shaw, M. L. G. (1982) PLANET: some experience in creating an integrated system for repertory grid applications on a microcomputer. *International Journal of Man–Machine Studies* **17**(3), 345–360.

Shaw, M. L. G. and Gaines, B. R. (1987) KITTEN: knowledge initiation and transfer tools for experts and novices. *International Journal of Man–Machine Studies* **27**(3), 251–280.

Skinner, B. F. (1965) *Science and Human Behaviour.* The Free Press, New York.

Sleeman, D. (1982) Assessing competence in basic algebra. In Sleeman, D. and Brown, J. S. (eds), *Intelligent Tutoring Systems*, pp. 185–199. Academic Press, London.

Sleeman, D. (1985) UMFE: a user modelling front-end subsystem. *International Journal of Man–Machine Studies* **23**(1), 71–88.

Sloman, A. (1983) *POPLOG: A Multi-purpose, Multi-Language Program Development Environment.* University of Sussex, Brighton.

Smith, S. F. (1984) Adaptive learning systems. In Forsyth, R. (ed.) *Expert Systems: Principles and Case Studies*, pp. 169–189. Chapman and Hall, Cambridge.

Smolensky, P., Monty, M. L. and Conway, E. (1984) Formalizing task descriptions for command specification and documentation. In Shackel, B. (ed.), *INTERACT '84*. Elsevier-North Holland, Amsterdam.

Sridharan, N. (1985) User modelling and plan recognition. In Sleeman, D. (ed.), *User Modelling Panel, Proceedings of IJCAI 1985, Los Angeles*, pp. 1298–1302.

Staddon, J. E. R. (1983) *Adaptive Behaviour and Learning*. Cambridge University Press, Cambridge.

Suchman, L. (1987) *Plans and Situated Actions*. Cambridge University Press, Cambridge.

Tannenbaum, A. S. (1989) *Computer Networks*, 2nd edn. Prentice Hall.

Tennant, H. R., Ross, K. M. and Thompson, C. W. (1983) Usable natural language interfaces through menu-based natural language understanding. *Proceedings CHI '83*, pp. 154–160.

Tennyson, R. D. *et al.* (1985) Adaptive control of learning time and content sequence in concept learning using computer based instruction. *Journal of Experimental Psychology* **77**(4), 218–222.

Thomas, J. C. and Schneider, M. L. (eds) (1984) *Human Factors in Computing Systems*. Ablex, Norwood, New Jersey.

Totterdell, P. A. and Cooper, P. A. (1986) Design and evaluation of the AID adaptive front end to Telecom Gold. In Harrison, M. D. and Monk, A. F. (eds), *People and Computers: Designing for Usability*. Cambridge University Press, Cambridge.

Totterdell, P. A., Norman, M. A. and Browne, D. P. (1987) Levels of adaptivity in interface design. In Bullinger, H. J. and Shackel, B. (eds), *Human Computer Interaction — INTERACT '87*, pp. 715–722. Elsevier-North Holland, Amsterdam.

Totterdell, P. A., Boyle, E., Mayes, T. and McEachen, P. (1989) Designing for user benefit—a methodological cautionary tale. *Ergonomics* **32**(11), 1469–1482.

Trevellyan, R. and Browne, D. P. (1987) A self-regulating adaptive system. *Proceedings CHI + GI '87 Conference on Human Factors in Computing Systems and Graphics Interface*, pp. 103–107.

Tulving, E. (1972) Episodic and semantic memory. In Tulving, E. and Donaldson, W. (eds), *Organization and Memory*. Academic Press, New York.

Tyler, S. W. and Treu, S. (1989) An interface architecture to provide adaptive task-specific context for the user. *International Journal of Man–Machine Studies* **30**(3), 303–328.

van der Veer, G. C., Tauber, M. J., Waern, Y. and van Muylwijk, B. (1985) On the interaction between system and user characteristics. *Behaviour and Information Technology* **4**(4), 289–308.

Viliunas, R. J., Wong, A. C. and Totterdell, P. A. (1988) Groupie: meeting a group's help needs. *Alvey Conference*.

Wahlster, W. and Kobsa, A. (1986) Dialog-based user models. In *Proceedings of the IEEE-74* (Special Issue on Natural Language Processing), pp. 948–960.

Walther, G. H., and O'Neill, H. F. (1974) On-line user computer interface—the effect of interface flexibility, terminal type, and experience on performance. *National Computer Conference*, pp. 379–384.

Wasserman, A. I. and Shewmake, D. T. (1984) The role of prototypes in the user software engineering (USE) methodology. In Hartson, H. R. (ed.), *Advances in Human Computer Interaction*. Ablex, San Francisco.

Watts, S. (1988) Expert software teaches air traffic controllers a lesson. *New Scientist*, 29 September, 40.

Wilcoxon, F. (1949) Some rapid approximate statistical procedures. American Cyanamid Co., Stanford, CT.

Wilensky, R., Arens, Y. and Chin, D. (1984) Talking to UNIX English: an overview of UC. *Communications of the ACM* **27**(6), 574–592.

Wilkinson, A. (1987) Using a genetic algorithm as the mechanism of adaptation in a self adapting interface. Unpublished MSc dissertation, Warwick University.

Wilkinson, B. (1983) *The Shopfloor Politics of New Technology*. Heinemann, London.

Wilson, S. W. (1986) Knowledge growth in an artificial animal. In Narandra, K. S. (ed.), *Adaptive learning systems*, pp. 247–253. Plenum Press, New York.

Witkin, H. A. and Goodenough, D. R. (1981) *Cognitive styles: Essence and Origin*. International University Press, New York.

Wong, A. C. B. and Lesan, H. (1988) Task organiser. Internal AID Report aid/3/report/s0234.1.

Woods, W. A. (1970) Transition network grammars for natural language analysis. *Communications of the ACM* **13**(10), 591–606.

Yates, F. E. (1984) Biological views of adaptation—some historical accounts. In Selfridge, O. G., Rissland, E. L. and Arbib, M. A. (eds), *Adaptive Control of Ill-Defined Systems*. Plenum Press, New York.

Zadeh, L. A. (1963) On the definition of adaptivity. *Proceedings of the IEEE* 469.

Zipf, G. K. (1949) *Human Behaviour and the Principle of Least Effort*. Addison Wesley, Ontario.

INDEX